Mike Minter:

Driven by Purpose…The Power of a Dream

God Bless!

Comfort PUBLISHING

All Scripture quotations, unless otherwise indicated, are taken from the Holy
Bible; New International Version.

First printing

Library of congress control Number 2008933323

Cover Design by Rana Matheson Robertson
Front Cover Photography by Kent Smith Photography
Back Cover Photography by Scott Stiles Photography

ISBN 978-09802051-0-7
PUBLISHED BY COMFORT PUBLISHING, LLC
www.comfortpublishing.com

Printed in the United States of America.

Also by Pamilla S. Tolen

Abram's Journey: Quest for the Man in the Stars
with Kimberly B. Brouillette

Abram's Journey: Quest for the Promise

Acknowledgement

To say that this book was a team effort would be an understatement. It was a collaboration by many people, who have a tremendous amount of talent, and I wish I could thank each one of them with long paragraphs of praise.

There are several of those people who do need to be recognized for their input and encouragement. The first of those people is James Warder, Vice-President of Acquisitions at Comfort Publishing. James spent months diligently editing the manuscript and adding input where he felt it was necessary to expand on the information presented. I am sincerely grateful for the hours he dedicated to this work and the suggestions he made to make it better. His efforts have honed my own writing skills and given me some new perspectives on writing styles.

In addition, I cannot fail to mention Kim Cassell and Carol Lynn Rorie who were also involved in editing the manuscript. Their efforts to make this work more enjoyable for the reader through proper punctuation are, I'm sure, applauded by everyone.

I would also like to thank Jason Huddle for his keen eye and knowledge of stats that caught even the minutest error in the scores and play-by-play descriptions of games mentioned in the book.

Finally, I would like to thank Mike Minter for the opportunity to write the story of a truly genuine man who loves Jesus and desires to tell his story to help others. After spending over nine months and countless hours with him in interviews, I can truly say that he is, in private life, the same person that the public embraces. It has been an honor to know and work with him, and I am thankful for having had that privilege.

Pamilla S. Tolen
July 27, 2008

In Loving Memory of

Florida Maye Minter

November 1946-August 2006

"For I know the plans I have for you, declares the LORD, plans to prosper you and not to harm you, plans to give you hope and a future. 12 Then you will call upon me and come and pray to me, and I will listen to you. 13 You will seek me and find me when you seek me with all your heart. 14 I will be found by you, declares the LORD, and will bring you back from captivity."

Jer 29:11-14 (NIV)

Mike Minter:

Driven by Purpose…The Power of a Dream

Chapter 1

DEFENSE IS THE BEST OFFENSE

*Sometimes life sticks its claws in you. How you prepare for
this attack could determine the final outcome.*

Over the years, I have found that life is a mixture of good days and bad days. This was a very bad day. This was the day we would bury Florida Maye Minter…my mother…my inspiration…my earthly rock. I could feel my heart beating. I could feel it in my chest, but it seemed so out of time with all that was going on around me. Until now, the biggest ache I felt was in my left knee. Although surgically repaired more than once, it hurt constantly to the point that I couldn't even straighten it out all the way. On this day, however, the pain in my knee was nothing compared to the ache in my heart.

I sat stiffly in a chair reserved for family members at the gravesite. As I looked around the cemetery, I was surprised to see so many people. Mama would definitely be pleased, I thought. My brother, Chewy, shifted awkwardly in the seat beside me. My sister, Boo, clutched a tissue already wet from her many tears. In fact, she held that tissue so tightly; I could almost see the veins standing up on the back of her hand. I knew that this one tissue could never hold all the grief she held inside.

A multitude of cousins stood close by. Their whispers filled the air as they spoke softly with one another. Seated near me, Mama's favorite nephew, Garfield Bowles, sat silently, listening. He had been blinded by a gunshot wound almost 25 years earlier and represented a somewhat darker side of the Alexander family.

Most of Mama's sisters and brothers had already passed before her, as well as her mother and dad. My uncle, Leonard Alexander, and aunt, Jean Bowles, Garfield's mother, were the last of her siblings. Still, there must have been five generations of our family that had come together to pay their last respects.

Among the others, I spotted Jerry Richardson, the owner of the Carolina Panthers, the NFL football team for whom I had played my entire career. He was accompanied by our head coach, John Fox, and our general manager, Marty Hurney. It was also a comfort to see Mike Rucker, the Panther's massive defensive-end and one of my best friends. I knew they were there out of respect for my mama...respect for the way she had raised me. I will never forget any of them for their honor and show of support at this lowest point of my life.

Only three of Mama's four children were able to be here, and that empty space left a lasting impression on me. Mama would have been saddened due to the circumstances that prevented her oldest child from saying goodbye for the last time. A DVD was to be made of the service so my sister, Lynn, could watch it from her prison cell in Texas.

The sun was hot, and beads of sweat danced on the brows of most of the observers. I was thankful that the canopy over the grave offered some protection, however little, from the sweltering Oklahoma heat. Nevertheless, I could feel the sweat seeping out of every pore in my body. I was still cold inside, bone-chilling cold. It reminded me of the first time I visited Nebraska. It was only 9 degrees Fahrenheit outside, and I did not even bring a coat with me. It was the void inside that I felt most though. I knew beyond any doubt the emptiness I felt today would last a long, long time.

The peacefulness of the moment prevailed until the sound of horses' hoofs and the crush of asphalt being trodden broke the silence. The carriage, drawn by six white horses, moved slowly as it transported Mama's coffin to the gravesite. Clop. Clop. Clop. Clop. It was the only sound heard throughout the entire area. The horses' burden was heavy, but they never faltered. Focused and determined, they moved closer and closer to their final destination. Mama had requested this type of send-off many times during her lifetime. It was an idea she got from watching one of her favorite movies, "Imitation of Life."

Mama's words echoed in my head, "Don't forget, you're my six million dollar man. You're going to be something special, Mike." I suppose she coined the phrase from a 1970s favorite television show of hers, staring Lee Majors. She had said it to me many times during my childhood.

As I waited for the pall-bearers to transport the casket to the bier, I thought about my life and the path it had taken. Did Mama's words set it all in motion? Did she send out instructions to supernatural forces in the universe? Were those words a driving force? Did they enable me to overcome difficulties that threatened to push me from my appointed destiny? Is it really possible to affect our own lives and those of others by the words we speak? There is no doubt in my mind that there is a relationship. But, in the end, it all comes down to responsible choices that solidify the framework of our individual lives.

I stared sadly at Mama's coffin as the pastor began to speak, eulogizing her in life and death.

Then, as if time had stood still, his hushed words of comfort ended. He was moving forward to shake our hands and to console us once more. The funeral was over, and we were left with only memories of times past...memories that reflected the essence of my mama and all that she had conveyed to each of us throughout her life.

I was 32 years old, and my life was in turmoil. After nine years playing NFL football for the Carolina Panthers, my career was coming to an end. I knew it. It was just a matter of time now. Maybe I would play two more years at the most, I reasoned. In the physical and violent world of professional football, I was an old man. My entire life, to this point, had been a process of reaching the dream I was living...of playing football at its highest level...of a career in the NFL. Now, I wondered what I was going to do with the rest of my life. At that very moment in time, when my mama's stabilizing influence was needed most, she was gone. I thought about her life and the choices she had made.

Florida Maye Minter was born in Altus, Oklahoma in 1946. She was the 12th child of a poor family who eventually made their way to Lawton,

Oklahoma sometime during the 1950s. Soon after her graduation from high school in 1965, Mama married a man named Cleo Sims. During their short marriage, she gave birth to two daughters, Karen, nicknamed Lynn, and Roselind, nicknamed Boo. Then, Cleo, along with my Uncle Leonard Alexander, was shot during a fight at a local nightclub. Each man sustained a gunshot wound to his leg, which required amputation. Cleo chose not to have his leg amputated. He died soon afterwards from blood poisoning. Uncle Leonard, by electing to amputate his limb, survived the ordeal. Choices these men made about their lives became a matter of life or death.

My sisters were very young when Cleo died and do not remember him at all. I reflected on this fact for a moment and realized that the choice Cleo made affected his entire family. It changed the course of my mama's life and those of his daughters.

In 1971, Mama married my dad, Michael Christopher Minter. Dad was in the military, stationed at Fort Sill, Oklahoma when Mama met him. The base had been established by General Philip Sheridan with the help of frontier scouts Buffalo Bill Cody and Wild Bill Hickok. Its purpose was to control raids into Texas and Kansas by the Native American tribes of the Kiowa, Comanche and Apache. For all intents and purposes, the fort is a suburb of Lawton, Oklahoma...or maybe it's the other way around. In any event, they are considered one and the same, which is evidenced by a a sign that says "Welcome to Lawton/Fort Sill."

After my father's tour of duty ended, my parents remained in Lawton for several years where Dad worked for the city. In Lawton, there were only three good jobs that a black person could aspire to-one was in the military, stationed at the army base; one was working for the Goodyear Company; and one was working for the city of Lawton. My dad had managed to attain two of those three jobs in his short time in Oklahoma. That was certainly an accomplishment.

In 1973, however, Dad decided that he wanted to move back to his hometown of Cleveland, Ohio. According to my Uncle Leonard, he just got homesick for his own family. Mama was not happy about his decision to move, but reluctantly went with him. As a result, there would be several changes in her lifestyle to which Mama would have to become accustomed. One was the fact that my dad was Catholic, and his family was very religious. Being a staunch Baptist, my Grandma Nettie was not at all enthusiastic about the move.

"What should we do about the girls?" Mama asked her mother. "I hate to move them in the middle of the school year."

"I think you should leave the girls with me," Grandma Nettie replied. "Once you get settled, they can go up there to live. There is no reason to disrupt their routines right now."

Grandma lived in an 800-square-foot duplex that was part of Lawton's government funded projects. She had lived in that same complex for many years with my grandfather and raised many of her 13 children and grandchildren from this modest two-bedroom home.

My Grandma Nettie, who was already 66 years old by the time I was born, had married a Baptist preacher named Tommy Alexander early in the 1920s. Upon their move to Lawton, he became the pastor of Calvary Baptist Church, where my family attended. After almost 50 years together, Tommy Alexander died in 1969 and left Grandma as the matriarch of our family.

Grandma was a care-taker by nature, and she wanted to keep her family close. I suspect she thought that if the girls remained with her, perhaps my mom and dad would return to Oklahoma to live in Lawton once again. My mom would prove to be cut from the same mold, and her life would reflect it. Her family was always a priority.

During the period that my mom and dad were living in Cleveland, my sisters, did, in fact, live with Grandma Nettie, along with two other cousins. My sister, Lynn, slept with our cousin, Donna. My cousin, Garfield, the only boy, had his own bed. That left Boo to share Grandma's bed. Boo once told me that Grandma Nettie got up at about 4 a.m. each morning and spent her first waking moments on her knees praying. Sometimes, Boo would pray along with her. Then, Grandma would read her Bible before beginning her daily chores. Her work included laying out all the children's clothing, feeding them and getting everyone off to school.

Soon after moving to Cleveland, my mom became pregnant, and I was born on January 15, 1974. Ironically, it was the seventh anniversary of the very first Super Bowl game between the Green Bay Packers and Kansas City Chiefs. How could anyone have possibly known that, 30 years later, I would take my place on that same stage, playing professional football. I was named after my father, Michael Christopher Minter, and was Mama's first son.

In August, 1974, my Aunt Joyce and Boo decided to visit us in Cleveland.

"I am so homesick, Joyce," Mama confided to one of her favorite sisters. "Mike is eight months old now, and no one in Lawton has seen him. He's growing up so fast."

"Why don't you come back with Boo and me for a visit?" Joyce replied.

"Mike can't leave his work," Florida said.

"Then you and little Mike should come back with us," Joyce said. "You don't have to stay long, and Lynn needs to see her mother. You can show off your new baby and let everyone know what's happening up here in the north."

"Let me talk to Mike, first," Florida responded. "I don't think he'll mind if I make a short trip back to Lawton."

My dad knew Mama was sad at being so far from her family, and he was glad that she had the opportunity to travel home with her sister.

"I'll be back soon," Florida assured Mike as she climbed aboard the Greyhound bus. "I'll miss you."

"Take care of my boy," Mike called back to her. "And hurry back. I'm lonely already."

Florida waved goodbye once more through the bus window as the bus moved out onto the street. According to my sister Boo, the two-day trip was long and tiring, especially with a baby, but Mama was anxious to go home. She would have endured an even longer trip, if necessary.

Nettie met Mama with a big hug and helped her settle in for a nice visit. Grandma was happy that Mama had married Michael. Mama's life had been in such turmoil after the death of the girls' father. It was a relief for her to see her daughter's life finally becoming more stabilized. After all, Mama was only 28. "That's too young to be a widow," Grandma had voiced on several occasions.

Mama had only been in Lawton a few days when the telephone rang. She watched as Grandma's face changed quickly from expectation to anguish as she handed her the telephone.

"Florida?" the voice on the other end questioned.

"Yes," Mama replied.

"This is Goldine Minter."

Mama recognized my dad's mother's voice immediately. "What's wrong?" she asked.

"Mike had a heart attack today." Goldine's voice shook, and she was crying. "He never recovered, Florida. Mike's dead. You need to come home immediately. We've already begun making arrangements with the priest for the funeral, but you need to come quickly."

Devastated, Mama dropped the phone and sat down on the couch, covering her face with her hands. Tears streamed down her cheeks.

"What's wrong, Mama?" seven-year-old Boo asked trying to console her. Mama hugged my sister tightly.

"Your stepdad went to heaven today," Florida explained. "Mama has to go back to Cleveland right away to make arrangements for the funeral."

"How come he didn't wait to say goodbye to us, Mama?" Boo asked.

"Sometimes it happens so fast, you don't have time to tell anyone. I'm sure he wanted to let us know. He just didn't have time," Mama explained to Boo.

Mama left immediately for Cleveland and my dad's funeral. Afterwards, she packed all of our belongings and returned to Lawton. She never went back to Cleveland, not even for a visit with my dad's family. I don't really know the reason. She never discussed it and I never asked. Regardless, I guess she never thought it was important for me to know my other grandparents. Consequently, I was a grown man before I ever knew anything about my dad, his life or his family. My childhood in Lawton, Oklahoma had officially begun.

Lawton is located about 90 miles southwest of Oklahoma City and was named for General Henry W. Lawton. Lawton had been a quartermaster at Fort Sill, and was involved in the pursuit and capture of legendary Apache Chief Geronimo. In later years he became a distinguished Spanish-American War hero. However, the town of Lawton was not actually founded until 1901 when the last of the Indian Lands in Oklahoma Territory, encompassing the Kiowa-Comanche-Apache land, was opened for settlement. Unlike earlier years in Oklahoma, there was no land rush to stake a claim. Instead, a lottery was held. It began in El Reno, Oklahoma, on July 29, 1901, where the order for filing the homestead claims was determined for three new towns in Oklahoma. Lawton was to be one of them. More than 100,000 people filed applications, but only 6,500 were chosen to receive land disbursed in 160 acre parcels around the purposed town of Lawton. A tract of 320 acres was reserved for the town site and sold at public auction. Consequently, on September 25, 1901, the Rock Island Railroad rolled in and the town was officially born.   By the 1970s, the population was about 70,000, and not a bad place for a boy to grow up.

"Hey Mike, I'm so sorry for your loss." A close friend of Mama brought my thoughts back to reality.

"Thanks," I said. "Yes, Mama will be sincerely missed by a lot of people around here."

Crowds of people still stood around the canopy that covered my mama's last resting place. Many of these people had not seen each other in a long time. This was obvious from the chatter, which conveyed information back and forth. As I eavesdropped, I looked across the cemetery at Gene Johnson. He looked so sad. I guess in some ways, he felt the loss of my mama as deeply as her own children.

My thoughts returned to the time when Mama was again alone, with three young children. I wondered if the sadness I felt now was anything close to how my mama felt when my dad died. I thought about her on-again, off-again relationship with Gene and the effect he'd had on my life. The first thing I remember about Gene was that he was always a sharp dresser. Wherever he went, he looked like somebody who was on his way to the top. When I was growing up, he drove a light blue Cadillac with a black, cloth roof and, by the standards of the neighborhood, he possessed the three things that made you somebody; he had a job with the city, he was a sharp dresser and he drove a sleek-bodied Cadillac. Gene was a tall man, although not powerfully built. You got a sense just by looking at him that this was a man not to be messed with. Today, he looked so much smaller. I asked myself, was he wondering what might have been under different circumstances?

After my dad's death, William Johnson, nicknamed Gene, had filled the void my mama intensely felt. He was an old friend from her high school years who consoled her in her grief. Soon afterwards, the friendship evolved into a romance.

Mama may have been impressed by him, but not my grandma. She did not like Gene at all and told him that she didn't want him hanging around her daughter. Grandma had a way of sizing people up and she was quick to speak her piece about him. Regardless, Mama continued the relationship, and the union produced another son, William, nicknamed "Chewy."

My eyes swept the grounds for Chewy. I spotted him talking to an old neighbor. Chewy was less than two years younger than me, and he became my "main man." We were inseparable from the time he was born until I finally left home. I was determined to be his protector and I never allowed anyone to take advantage of my little brother. Even today, I feel the same about him and my whole family.

As I sat by Mama's grave in the midday heat, a sharp pain caused me to begin weeping again. It wasn't a physical pain. It was the hurt that goes to the very depth of your soul…it makes your stomach churn…and it sits on your chest like a 350-pound offensive lineman, just squeezing the very life out of you. As I wiped my eyes, I thought about Lynn, sitting in a prison cell in Texas. I knew she was thinking about us. I could feel it. Boo, Chewy and I had gone to visit her just days before the funeral. I was amazed at what had happened to the sister I had not seen for almost 20 years.

Prison is a harsh and unforgiving environment, and the lifestyle that Lynn had chosen so early in her life was evidenced by the lines on her face as she spent time with us that day. What do you say to someone who you were so close to early in your life and whose life is now so alien to your own? In that large room, with rows of chairs and folding tables set aside for the visitors of the inmates who must be kept away from the rest of society, we laughed and reminisced about times long ago that we had all shared together.

One of those times revolved around the many weekends and summers spent with Grandma. In fact, my earliest memories center around my grandmother and the strong spirit of love that was so evident to each member of her family. It was my grandmother who introduced me to God. Her unfaltering beliefs and constant encouragement about the need for God in my life remain with me even today as I raise my own children. I remember, vividly, the times she would patiently listen as I told her all the things I had done that day. She always seemed so interested in what a five-year-old boy had to say to her.

The whole Alexander family spent so much time at my grandmother's that my role models became my mama's 13 siblings and my 25 cousins. I figure that at least three generations of our family stayed in that tiny home at one time or another. In fact, there were so many children together in her house at one time that it was only natural that a "pecking order" would develop. This situation led to one of the first lessons I learned in life, which was defense.

"Remember the cats?" I said to Lynn, trying to lighten the mood. "You were so beautiful and had such an unusual ability to organize people and form alliances with the cousins."

Lynn laughed and put her head back, thinking about the more carefree times in her life.

Lynn had been a natural leader and proved it on many occasions. To this day…to this very moment…it saddens me knowing that choices she had made at such an early age would have such a negative impact on the rest of her life. Her personality was so dynamic that, many times, some of my cousins would be completely distraught because Lynn was mad at them.

"If a kid was in your group, they were perceived as cool," I said jokingly. "All of the rest of us were targets."

"You go on," Lynn replied, seeming to find some sort of comfort in recalling better times.

"I remember that since I was one of the younger children, I was constantly being put in the position of defending myself. That crazy deal with the cats created a fear that has followed me into my adult life. Did you know that?" I asked her.

"What?" Lynn replied. "What are you talkin' about?"

"I developed a very deep fear of cats," I repeated. "Remember when Grandma kept all those alley cats? I guess she used them to chase away the mice. The cats would congregate together. Some of them were as big as a dog. Many times there would be 10 to 15 in one place.

Just then, Boo laughed, and I knew then that she too was recalling a very special memory as I began to relate the rest of the story.

"I remember that once there was a possum up in our tree, and all those cats were circling underneath just waiting to catch that possum. Now, I knew that these cats were very sneaky. It's easy to tell when a dog is coming at you and, when they do, you can react to the situation. A cat, though, will pounce on you when you least expect it and scratch you on your neck. At least this was my perception as a four-year-old boy.

I stopped the story when my eye caught the movement of the prison guard who was surveying the various visitors that day. Then, I proceeded with my tale.

"Now, Lynn," I looked directly at her for effect, "and her foot soldiers, the older cousins, were very aware that all of us little kids were afraid of those cats. You would wait until we were in bed, sound asleep, and bring the cats in and throw them on us.

We all began to chuckle at the visual image I was creating with this story. "The cats, I'm sure, were just as frightened as we were. So, wherever they landed, they attached themselves securely with their claws. We had scratches and bites everywhere. That was not nice, Lynn," I concluded.

"You don't fool me, Mike," Lynn said, chiding me. "You figured it out and weren't even in the bed."

I had to admit that I remembered, vividly, lying in Grandma's bed at night as a young boy. The room was small, with no frills, housing only a double bed and long dresser. There were no lamps and the only light for the room came from the ceiling fixture that, when turned on, cast eerie shadows on the wall. A small closet with bi-fold doors provided additional storage space.

The cool darkness felt wonderful as I scooted further under the covers. I visualized the scene once more. I was listening intently for sounds from the hallway that foretold of a coming chaos. Beside me, the other children were already asleep.

"Shh," Lynn's voice whispered outside the bedroom door. "You'll wake them up."

My ears strained to distinguish what my sister was saying to the other children with her.

"Meow!" The muffled voice of a cat rang out.

She must have it under her sweater, I thought. I better hurry or they'll be in here before I can get away. Someone behind the closed bedroom door was snickering. Hurry, Mike, I thought as I slipped from beneath the covers and tiptoed quickly to the closet. I had just settled myself amongst the clothes and other items that secured my hiding place when the door suddenly sprung open, and giggling children rushed in to unload several cats on the sleeping children still in bed.

"Meoooooooow!" the cats screeched as the terrified children screamed.

More giggling, as the intruders vanished down the long hallway and into the night, while the adults rushed into the bedroom to comfort crying children.

It was an interesting phenomenon to me, as I watched this scene played out time after time. First, there were the little children my age, who were able to sleep, knowing full well what might happen. Then, there were the older children, guided by their ring-leader, General Lynn, who never seemed to tire of inflicting the same fear, over and over, on their unsuspecting prey.

In my young mind, I began to see patterns and realized that people are creatures of habit. Knowing this information would become invaluable to me when I played football. So, very early in my life I began to understand that sometimes a strategy was needed to give me an advantage. I was not always the strongest competitor, but I began to recognize that the best defense was not necessarily brute strength; rather, it was to anticipate my opponent, and take action before he did.

In life I have found that there is no better strategy for overcoming difficulties than to have a defender who is always there to watch your back. For me, my advocate is Jesus Christ.

Still sitting uncomfortably in the grayness that dominates everything that defines a prison, I nodded to Lynn. "You're right, but it still has its effect on me, even today. I guess I still have a ways to go. You know, as I grew older, my fear never lessened. I remember one night, when I was in college, I was at my friend's house playing cards. They had a cat, but they put it outside while I was visiting. On one occasion, one of the children left the door open and the cat got inside. I was in the middle of the game, looking at my cards, when that cat jumped up on my lap. Man, I just panicked! I couldn't move. I used to watch movies where people were put in situations where they were just paralyzed by fear, and I would be hollering at them 'Get up! You can move!' Then, it happened to me. My hands were in the air and I was screaming, 'Get that cat off me.'"

Just like in the movies, except for my waving hands, I was totally paralyzed. I couldn't even look down. I was afraid to look because I've always believed that when you look something in the eye, it's either going to retreat or it's going to come after you. In my mind, cats are always going to come after you. To this day, I'm still afraid of small cats, and it's all because of you," I said staring directly at Lynn.

At this point we were all laughing uncontrollably, and I guess I was laughing hardest of all.

At just that moment, something else struck Boo as especially funny. "It was very ironic that your whole football career was with the Carolina Panthers," she said.

"I love the big cats, though. I'm fascinated by the power and strength of a lion or a panther. It's crazy, but I'm scared of the little ones," I said.

By then, visiting hours were over and Boo, Chewy and I stood up to go.

"You'll be out soon," I said to my older sister. "Don't forget you still have family that cares about you."

"I won't forget," Lynn said sadly. "I'm so sorry. I just wish I could be there for Mama."

"I know," I said. "She knows how you feel though, and in one way, you will be there."

"Bye," the three of us said almost in unison. "Take care now."

"I will," Lynn replied with a slight smile on her drawn face.

Suddenly, the smell of flowers caught my attention, and my mind snapped back to reality. There were so many of them, and I recalled how Mama had loved flowers. The thought made me smile again. People were still milling around but there weren't as many as there were earlier. I saw the attendants from the funeral home standing by the hearse. They looked impatient for everyone to leave so they could complete their work and go home.

"Are we all meeting at Mama's house?" Chewy asked. He had seen me and was walking towards me.

"Yes," I said. "Kim has already taken the kids there and is waiting on me."

"I think they're ready for us to leave," Chewy said, pointing to the family car. Boo was already seated. I knew she must be anxious to get back to all the people who would be coming to the house to talk and eat. Chewy and I walked slowly towards the car. I looked at the names engraved on all the copper plates arranged in neat lines across the ground. I wondered how many of those people Mama had known

We settled into our seats and the car slowly moved toward the Highland Cemetery exit. My eyes were fixed on Mama's coffin and I couldn't keep the tears from beginning once more. As the car pulled onto the highway, my thoughts again returned to the Panthers and what the near future held for me. There would be a lot of decisions to make shortly, but, for now, all of that was put on the backburner. I was determined to play my heart out for Mama during the 2006 football season. At least I could do that one last thing for her.

As the family car moved toward Mama's house, I looked out the car window at the place that had been such an integral part of my life. We passed a green house on the corner of one street, and I was once again lost in a sea of early memories.

They began when I was about three or four, when our family moved to a small green house at 2422 Washington Street. The street was located in an area of town that most people would call the other side of the tracks. As an adult looking back on my life, I saw now how rundown and dirty this area really was.

The house had belonged to Gene's mother. It had a carport and there was a big pear tree in the front yard. There was also a fence around the yard and a tree near the fence where we had put up a makeshift basketball rim. We had taken a bicycle tire rim and knocked out all the spokes and nailed it on the tree so we could play basketball. Even now, I'm still amazed at how resourceful we were when it came to getting what we wanted.

There was a front lawn, but, as you rounded the back of the house, the tall grass and weeds made it impossible to walk around. A long-forgotten swimming pool, filled in with dirt and weeds, was evidence that at one time this house was very special to some previous owner. I don't think the grass in the backyard was ever cut. We cut the front once or twice a year, maybe.

There was no porch and the front door brought you immediately into the living room. The kitchen was separated from the living room by a half-wall. Three bedrooms were located down the hallway to the right. The bedroom farthest down the hall was Mama's. The middle one belonged to the girls and the bedroom closest to the kitchen was where Chewy and I slept.

It wasn't a large house, but, to me, it was a mansion. I guess the Washington Street house will always be special to me because it was the place where I began to develop my imagination.

Chewy and I would ball up socks and pretend that they were footballs, and the furniture represented people who were trying to prevent us from scoring touchdowns. We would dive over the couch, pretending to jump over a defender in order to score. Sometimes, I convinced Chewy to run so I could tackle him. I would tackle him so hard that we put dents and holes in the living room wall. Mama would get so mad at our rough-housing. I never understood why she was so upset. After all, we were just playing and the walls had seen so much abuse I wondered how she even noticed our part in the destruction. Then, she would leave the room and I would somehow convince Chewy to get up and let me tackle him all over again.

"Run for a pass, Chewy," I would say as I threw the ball in the air. Chewy would respond accordingly. Then, the minute he caught the ball I was pounding him into the couch, or chair or wall.

Boom! The sound would once again bring Mama back into the room.

"Boys!" Mama hollered. "I'm not putting up with this anymore! You boys take it outside right now!" Now that I have children of my own, I understand why Mama was so angry. But, that was not the case when I was seven years old.

I cannot remember a time when I was not absorbed in football. Even as early as five and six years old, I was fascinated by the game. One of my cousins had played football at Lawton High, and I remember sitting in the bleachers with my five-year-old brother, watching the game. Chewy and I shared everything together, including a love of the game…football.

"Chewy," I said, "I'm going to play football on this field one day." It was at this time in my life that I began to dream about playing for the National Football League (NFL). Back then, the Dallas Cowboys were my team. One day I made a prediction. "I am going to play for the Cowboys and, with me on the team, we will win the Super Bowl!"

Imagination is such a powerful tool. It can take you places that can change your whole life. That's why it is so important for children to have their imaginations ignited with positive goals. It was through His imagination that God created the world and everything in it. Were it not for imagination, mankind would have never walked on the moon or paved the way to a cure for many dreaded diseases of our day. Imagination allowed me to dream, and those dreams ultimately became my reality.

But, imagination also taught me how to protect my turf, which was essential for survival in the neighborhood in which I grew up. In my mind, I would plan out a variety of challenges in which I might find myself. Then, I would decide, in advance, what action I was going to take to deal with the situation. Almost none of the solutions included diplomacy. Rather, the better answer was to get in the first lick before someone else beat you to it. I have to admit, though, that my sister, Boo, was also very instrumental in helping me learn to survive and gain respect. In fact, she even helped me win my first fight.

There was a kid that lived across the street from us. He was bigger than I was, and he kept picking on me. I remember thinking I didn't want to fight this boy. At this point in my life, avoiding pain was a main goal of daily life, and I just knew that if I had to fight this boy, I was in for some serious pain.

One day, he wrestled me to the ground saying, "Boy, I'm going to beat you up." I didn't say anything, because I was scared. When I went home the whole thing just ate at me. I felt like a chicken and that was especially painful because in our family, we were taught not to be scared of anything...we were taught to stand our ground and either dish out a beating or take a beating...but, above all, we were taught not to run away, Nevertheless, I had allowed this guy to get the better of me.

When this whole thing came down, Chewy was with me and he went to Boo and said, "This big boy was messing with Mike and wanted to beat him up." As Chewy tells it, Boo got really mad and said, "Nobody messes with my brother."

Not too long afterwards, we were sitting in our front yard. Garfield was there with us and he started instigating a fight. He called out across the street to the other house, "Bring that boy out here right now, and we'll whup him. Nobody's gonna beat up on my cousin."

Now, you have to realize that Garfield was older, and sometimes he would initiate a fight between the younger cousins. His reasoning was that we had to learn to be tough and that we needed to practice on each other. In an odd sort of way, Garfield taught us a sense of loyalty. This particular day, though, the fight would be with an outsider, and I was the guinea pig.

Garfield said to me, "Mike, get out there and show that boy what our family's made of." Then he proceeded to send me out into the street to beat the guy up. But, I was still a little guy and this boy was a big brute. I stood there, hesitantly, trying to decide what to do. I thought, what are you talking about? I don't want to fight this boy, he's bigger than me. That whole pain avoidance thing was taking over again.

Then Boo said to me, "I'll walk you out there."

So, the boy had one of his cousins walk him to the middle of the street, and Boo walked me to the street. I wondered to myself, how in the world am I going to beat this big dude? I didn't know. I just froze up. Then, all of a sudden, Boo got behind me and took my hands and started swinging. My body wasn't moving and I wasn't doing anything...at least not on my own.

"Don't you go talking trash to my brother," Boo screamed at the boy, immediately instilling fear or anger. I'm not sure which emotion he felt most. "Take this and this," she continued to chide. Using my hands and her skill, the poor boy was beaten to a frazzle and I came out the victor. I don't believe he got in even one punch.

Then the boy's cousin began yelling at Boo. "You can't get in this," he screamed.

"I'm not in it, I'm just holding his hands," Boo yelled back.

I was winning when the boy's cousin broke up the fight and even though my sister was really the one doing the fighting, that victory gave me a whole lot of confidence. That's how our family is, even today. We always look out for each other. By the way, I never had any problem with that boy after that.

The Alexander family had developed a name for themselves over the years. You didn't mess with us, or we would all come after you. That scenario would be proven over and over again in the coming years.

At that time, my sister, Lynn, was still living at home. I was in the third grade when Lynn starting running around with a lot of bad people. Mama didn't like it, and she and Lynn got into some knock-down, drag-out fights over Lynn's friends. Lynn would run away, then come home, and then, suddenly leave again. Mama was devastated by Lynn's actions, but she was helpless to do anything about it. At 17 years old, Lynn had already become the defiant teenager, who would eventually be led down a path that she did not want to go. During the period that Lynn was at home, she was the one who would discipline us. Lynn would wait until Mama left for work, then she would get a switch off the tree and whip Chewy and me for whatever transgressions we had committed. She wouldn't let us go outside because she wanted us to clean up the house, take the trash out, comb our hair and brush our teeth. We didn't want to do all that…what little boy does? We wanted to go outside and play with our friends. She was definitely trying to teach us discipline, but we weren't buying any of it. We would wait impatiently for Mama's black Cougar to come up our street. As soon as we saw her drive up to the house, we started acting up all over again. Mama didn't realize it, but she was our savior and protector.

Boo is two years younger than Lynn, seven years older than me and nine years older than Chewy. At 15, she became our second mom. She has always considered herself to be our protector and, whenever we needed support or a cheerleader, she was there as a believer in our dreams.

"Fear made me quit when I could have gone to college on a track scholarship," Boo once told us. "Fear can keep you from your dreams. I won't let that happen to either of you. Not while I have anything to say about it!"

Boo was the older voice in our lives, and she taught us how to become men. She instructed us about how to treat girls and how to respect other people. She became our conscience when we needed one. She made sure that Chewy and I experienced everything that she had missed. It was Boo that taught us how to apply, to real life, all the things we learned from Mama. Sometimes, an older, more experienced voice is necessary to be that encouragement you need in tough situations, even if that voice is your sister's.

As we left the cemetery that day, I found myself looking out the window as I continued to reflect on my life in Lawton. The car was slowing down, and I looked to see where we were. I didn't even recognize the area. Lawton had expanded so much since I had left home. How long had it been? I began to count backward. Ah yes, almost fifteen years. Wow! How can time pass so fast? How long since Grandma died? About 26 years, I guessed. It was the last time I could remember feeling such a desperate loss in my life.

Grandma Nettie Bell Alexander had passed away when I was six years old. Since I was still a small child, the strange circumstances surrounding her death are known to me mainly by family stories that have been retold many times. The best way I know how to explain it is by saying that some of my grandmother's children and grandchildren tended to align themselves on the wrong side of the law. Garfield definitely fit into that category. Many of my family referred to him as a "gangster," and he was the subject of a good deal of prayer in our house. When grandma was alive, she took him to church regularly, and he even sang in the choir. But my cousin seemed to march to a different drummer. At first, he was just a menace, setting grass fires and participating in various delinquent activities. As he grew older, though, he graduated to...shall we say...more lucrative forms of illegal activity, which eventually landed him in prison.

I remember, once, that Garfield and his buddies robbed a liquor store and stashed the liquor they stole in the closet of the bedroom Chewy and I shared on Washington Street. One day, we were playing in our room and we discovered the liquor, along with several guns. Chewy wanted to play with the guns, but I knew that Garfield would pound us good if he caught us. Garfield was well-known for hurting people who got in his way. Perhaps it was this reputation that proved to be Garfield's undoing.

On one particular occasion, a boy in our neighborhood crossed him and word spread that Garfield was out to get him. The boy knew that meant sure death, and he was scared. One day, Garfield, along with a friend went looking for the boy, who had been spotted at a local park. So Garfield drove there and parked. Before he could get out, the boy walked up to Garfield's side of the car. He was pointing a gun through the window, and Garfield looked directly at him.

Without showing an ounce of fear, Garfield laughed, "You won't shoot me. In fact, I dare you to shoot me. You know why I know you won't shoot that gun at me?" Garfield challenged the boy. "You won't shoot me because you don't have the balls to do it. In fact," Garfield continued, "I'm going to take that gun away from you right now and beat you within an inch of your life."

The boy stood his ground, biding his time as he considered his options. Then he heard a sound that sent fear through every inch of his body.

Click. It was the sound a car door opening. The boy knew he must make his decision now. Should he run for his life or stand and fight?

In an instant, the decision was made, and the shaking hand of the boy squeezed the trigger. A resounding explosion tore through the open window, shattering Garfield's face.

My grandmother was at home when she received a telephone call that informed her of the shooting and that Garfield was not expected to survive. Distraught, she fell to her knees screaming,

"Please God, take me instead," she pleaded. "Let him live."

Perhaps God answered her prayer, or maybe it was simply her time to die. No one can know for sure. Heartbroken, Grandma Nettie had a heart attack. She was taken immediately to the local hospital. It was the same hospital where Garfield lay near death. However, she never recovered and passed away a few days later in March, 1980. My cousin lost his eyesight but recovered and remains alive today.

The same spirit of love that I always felt from my grandmother was in my mama, too. No one in our family was without a place to stay if they needed one. Like Grandma, Mama was always ready to help someone in need. In spite of the fact that Cousin Garfield's activities were associated with bringing about my grandmother's death, Mom opened up our home for him to stay for short time. She and Boo even took him to the doctor for his frequent visits. After all, he was family and family took care of each other.

Grandma Nettie's funeral was heart-wrenching. I remember seeing my mama, aunts, uncles and cousins grieving uncontrollably. Many were unwilling to allow the casket to be closed and allow Grandma's body to be lowered into the ground. It was the first tragedy that I can remember and through it, I saw its effect on people. However, in spite of her sacrifice and the loss everyone felt, the message Grandma had tried so hard to impress on her family was eventually forgotten. Her desire that God be center of our family seemed to fade away.

Following Grandma's death, everyone began to gather at my aunt's house on the weekends. They tended to stay away from the local nightclubs because of all the fights that occurred there. I suppose it was also the result of Cleo and Uncle Leonard's unfortunate mishap. The adults seemed to enjoy getting together to discuss family issues. Mama never drank alcohol during the work week, but, on the weekend, it was her escape from the realities of her life. Sometimes those discussions resulted in fights among themselves. While they partied and talked, Chewy and I watched television in the back room with the other children. I still remember the many nights Chewy and I went to bed at my aunt's house, only to be awakened in the middle of the night and dragged home and into the cold night air because of some disagreement amongst the adults. Later, when Boo was old enough to take care of us alone, Chewy and I stayed at home with her. She didn't want to be there, and neither did we.

As the memories began to fade, I realized that, throughout the service, I felt as if I was walking in a fog...not to be connected to this earth of ours. I was aware of being at the funeral, yet it all seemed so surreal...kind of like an out-of-body experience. In football, they call it "being in the zone." You play the game, but you really don't recall the individual plays because of the intensity of it all. For me, that's what Mama's funeral was like. However, unlike football, there was no particular jubilation other than the fact that I knew Mama was in a better place. But, for me, there was just a deep, deep hole in my heart.

My eye caught the image of a small boy headed into a neighborhood convenience store. I could tell by the way he looked over his shoulder, motioning to his friends, what he intended to do. I wanted to stop the car and go after him. "Wait!" I wanted to cry out. "There's a better way. I know because I've been where you are."

Chapter 2

LEADER OF THE PACK

Sometimes, you get a second chance to do what's right.
You're wise to make the most of that opportunity.

I'm not sure when it began, but, it was before Grandma passed away. I had fallen into a pattern of that was accepted as normal by many of the children in my neighborhood. To be perfectly honest, we used to steal a lot. We would frequently go into a convenience store and take candy and other snacks. We never went hungry so I can't say that we had a need to steal in order to eat. Besides, we were taking candy and pop, things that all kids want but can't always have. However, one particular time, we went into a store and I was actually going to pay for a soft drink. I picked out a cold Pepsi from the refrigerator containing drinks, but it slipped out of my hand and smashed on the hard floor. I stood fixed in the isle and slowly looked up into the eyes of the clerk who was staring at me.

"You're going to have to pay for that," he said.

"No I'm not," I protested. "It was an accident. I didn't mean to break it."

"It doesn't matter. You dropped it, so you're responsible," the clerk countered. I looked at his eyes, and, at that moment, realized that he was ready to come around that counter and grab me, so I took off running. I ran down the aisle and out the door before he could get around the counter to catch me. As I ran into the parking lot, I was surprised by the fact that the clerk had followed me out of the store. I was running down the street trying to look behind to see if the guy was still chasing me. He was, so I started zigzagging through a maze of storage units that stood one street over from my house. I was hoping to slow him down. When I finally reached my street, I hid behind a car to see if he was still following me. At some point, during all the zigzagging, I guess he ran out of steam and quit.

Chewy had been in the store with me and watched the whole event unfold. When the clerk ran out of the store after me, he could have easily stolen anything in the store, but he didn't. He was so mesmerized, watching the man chase me that he just stood there. Eventually, before the man returned, he left and came looking for me.

For me, this was another lesson learned. It was the first time that I realized how fast I could run. Here I was, a six year old boy, and I outran a man that had legs twice as long as mine.

Another incident, proved to be my downfall in my life of crime, but it also changed my life. Chewy, I and some of our friends were doing what just came naturally for a bunch of youngsters…we were sitting on the lawn in front of our house and plotting our next great adventure…legal or not.

"I've been wanting some new Star Wars figures," Rerun said.

"Me too," Chewy replied.

"Let's go to Gibson's and see what they've got," Rocky chimed in.

"How are we going to get them out of the store?" Chewy questioned. "They'll see a bunch of us coming in together and suspect us right away. You know how the police are. Those store people are just the same."

We all sat silently for a moment, each trying to devise a solution to this problem in our own minds.

"I've got an idea," I said finally.

The other boys looked up expectantly. "What?" some of the group said in unison.

"What if we take off our shirts and walk in with them balled up. Then, we'll hide the toys in our shirts and walk casually out of the store."

"You don't think they'll suspect us?" Rocky laughed at the thought of a group of nappy haired black boys walking into a store together.

"Naw," I said confidently. "We won't have our shirts on. They'll just think we don't have anywhere to hide anything. They won't even notice our shirts balled up in our hands.

The group considered the plan, and all agreed it was worth a try, so we left for the store.

We grabbed our bikes and rode two to a bike to Gibson's, a local department store chain similar to Wal-Mart. Once inside, we each ambled up and down the aisles. It was a routine with us that we had acted out many times. Sometimes we came to the store just to scout it out. This time, however, I knew that our plan had precision and the store would be an easy mark.

Everyone split up and I made my way to my intended goal, the toy department, trying my best not to attract attention. As I walked through the isle labeled boys 7-14, I barely noticed the neat stacks of jeans, piled high on the display tables. My sole focus was the isle where action figures were located between games and large model trucks for boys my age and older. As I approached the isle I immediately saw the rack of GI Joe figures. Just below them the shelves were neatly stacked with every kind of Transformer I could imagine. Maybe some other time, I thought as I grabbed a storm trooper Star Wars action figure from the rack and quickly stuck it into the folds of my shirt. As I did this, I moved casually toward the front of the store, but when I arrived at the door, the looming figure of a security guard stood before me, blocking my exit.

"You steal something, boy?" he asked in a rhetorical manner.

"No sir," I replied in my most convincing voice.

"Let me see that shirt," he replied as he reached his hand out.

In an instant, and remembering that I had already proven faster than a fully-grown man in a foot race, I disappeared around a counter and down an aisle where stacks of clothes sat neatly piled on a table. The guard was close behind me but not close enough to see me throw the figure into the pile of clothes. As he rounded the corner, I stood there innocently waiting to show him my empty shirt. That should do it, I thought. Amazingly, he never asked for the shirt but began looking through the clothes until he retrieved the toy.

Holding it up for me to see, he asked, "This what you took?"

"Naw," I protested. "I didn't put that there."

"Come with me," he said, dragging me to the back of the store and further and further away from freedom. Son, my name is Mr. Calvert and I want you to sit down here, and don't move." He pointed towards a chair. Then he went out of the room and I was left alone to reflect on my fate. As I waited, my eyes surveyed the multitude of cameras that allowed the guard to see every corner of the store. I saw my brother and all my cousins leaving, and my heart sank. They had left me all alone in this store and now I was going to jail, I thought, beginning to panic.

Then, the security guard returned with his supervisor who said to me, "Son, do you know what you were doing?"

I just played dumb and said, "No."

He said, "You were stealing and you can go to jail for that. You know this could go on your record forever and it will never come off."

The thought struck me that everyone would know what I did, and if I went to jail, I wouldn't be able to play football. My heart was pounding and I felt like I wanted to throw up. "Michael Christopher Minter-that name could be blemished forever if I put this on your record," he continued. "But, I'm not going to put it on your record. I'm going to let you go. But you'd better never do this again. If I catch you back in this store stealing, I'm going to call the police. Do you understand?" the supervisor asked.

I was crying and my nose was running and, as I wiped my nose on my arm, I said, "I promise you I won't ever steal anything else again. Thank you, sir." From that point on, I never picked up another thing that wasn't mine. That conversation definitely made an impression on me. He had scared me straight. I was out of that store in a heartbeat, and I ran all the way home.

"Why did you guys leave me," I asked when I finally caught up with the group.

"We didn't want to get caught too," Rocky replied. "It was a dumb idea anyway."

I didn't actually realize it at the time, but that comment rang true with what President John F. Kennedy had said about 20 years earlier…that success has many fathers, and failure is an orphan…and my friends, who had so readily agreed to the idea of stealing from the store, were more than ready to blame me for its failure. Year later, my sister, Lynn, certainly felt the full brunt of that statement when she was accused of murder by the people she called her friends.

The next day was Easter Sunday, and I was sitting in the third row of pews at Calvary Baptist Church, waiting for the service to begin. Finally, the organist began to play as I fidgeted and quietly looked around to see who was late this time. My attention was immediately drawn by the sound of a familiar voice. Mr. Calvert, who I later learned was a deacon at our church, was standing at the pulpit to give an introductory message.

"You know, the Bible talks a lot about stealing," he was saying to the congregation. "Not only is it bad because you can get caught and go to jail," he continued, "but it isn't right to take something that doesn't belong to you. When you steal from a store, it's the same as if you stole something from an individual person."

I couldn't believe my eyes. I had never put it all together because this man looked a whole lot different in his guard's uniform than he did in his Sunday clothes. Mr. Calvert was the security guard who had caught me stealing at Gibson's store. Then, as if adding salt to the pain of my already wounded ego, the pastor got up and began his sermon about why people do the things they do, and how Jesus Christ came to take us away from all that.

I looked up and directly into the eyes of the man speaking. The pupils of my eyes must have doubled in size and I audibly caught my breath. Sweat began to trickle down my forehead, and I suddenly realized how dry my mouth had become. I just knew that Mr. Calvert had told the preacher what I had done. I knew that at any moment, this man was going to point his finger at me and say,

"And this young man, right there, is a prime example of what I am talking about. If anyone should know that it's wrong, it should be the grandson of one our former pastors, Tommy Alexander, God rest his soul."

I slid a little further down in my seat, refusing to look up. I was waiting for the wrath of God to come crashing down around my head and pulverize me on the spot. In my mind, I saw the eyes of Grandpa Tommy staring straight at me from his mansion in Heaven, shaking his head.

"How could such a good boy go so wrong," I could hear him thinking. "I thought he knew better then that!" As I glanced over to my grandmother sitting beside me, I honestly thought I heard her audibly sigh with despair.

I just knew for sure that the pastor was going to spill the beans, and Mama along with all my aunts and uncles and Grandma, would know what I had done. I was so embarrassed. In my mind, I began to bargain with the Lord. "Please, God, don't let him tell anyone about me. I promise I'll never steal another thing from anyone. Please, God! Please!"

The pastor's message finally ended, and the organ music introducing the final hymn began. "Thank you, God," I sighed quietly and let out a huge mass of air from my lungs. It was a lesson I will never forget, and I never did steal anything again. I had made yet another choice that would set the direction for the rest of my life.

In my third grade year, I was finally old enough to play football on a team. Most elementary schools in Oklahoma had teams, but my school, Bishop, could not afford one. The school compensated for this by signing students up for the local Boys Club team. (It was not called Boys and Girls Clubs until later.)

I was nine years old, and I felt a rush of excitement as I sat on the bench waiting for Coach Russell to pass out the gear. I had waited more then two years and was impatient to finally begin practice.

"Mike," my balding coach bellowed. "Come get your equipment and suit up." He was a big man, at least to a nine year old.

I walked confidently towards the coach as he handed me my uniform. In the locker room, however, as I held the pads up, surveying them from every angle, I looked up to find Coach monitoring my progress.

"Need help with those pads, Minter?" he asked.

I was reluctant to hand them to him, slightly embarrassed that the beginning of my football career required instruction on how to dress properly for the game. I was also a bit concerned that if I gave them up, he might not give them back.

That week I will always remember as one of the most exciting times in my life. I was finally on a real football team, and I could prove it. I had a jersey with a number on it. I wore that jersey every day until the first big game. I don't think I even allowed my mama to wash it. I think I even slept in it. I was so proud of being on a team. I had begun the trip towards my destiny and I was ready to arrive at my destination as fast as possible.

In a city that is home to a majority of blue-collar workers, sports are the uniting force that dominates leisure activities. Almost every school had a football and basketball team, even in the elementary grades. If a school in Lawton, such as my first school, Bishop, could not afford one, then the local Boys Club became the answer. Championship games were the rallying point for all the citizens. In a town where white people and other races and cultures were still emotionally segregated from each other, sports were the unifying factor that brought them all together.

The stadium where the city championship games were held seated about 10,000 people and, during those games, every seat was filled with spectators watching with anticipation, hoping their teams would win. It was in this stadium of cheering fans, screaming at the top of their lungs for victory, that I first experienced the "thrill of victory and agony of defeat," which for decades was sports announcer, Jim McCay's, trademark opening for ABC's Wide World of Sports.

I will never forget the exhilaration of being on a winning team, whose hopes were eventually dashed by the agony of the one loss that kept us from being the champions. That year, we won every game except one. Douglas Elementary, which went on to the city championship, beat us in a 6-0 victory. It was the only stain on a perfect record. I must have cried for three days over that loss. That's also when I first came to understand that there is no satisfaction with second place in sports or in life.

We moved to another house in the Country Club area of Lawton my fourth grade year. This area was only about a 30 minutes drive from where we had lived on Washington Street, but that 30 minutes represented a gulf that was as vast as the East is from the West. It was definitely a move in the right direction. The housing was much nicer and neighborhoods were cleaner. Plus it was a long way from an area of town designated "The Hill," where all the prostitution and drug buys now took place. The move also necessitated a change in schools, and Chewy and I were excited that the school we were going to attend in the fall had its own football team. However, moving to a different neighborhood brought with it a new set of challenges as well as opportunities. On Washington Street, I had become the unquestioned leader of our group, and I liked that role. Now, I would need to reestablish that role for myself with an entirely new group of boys.

It was summer, and the days were lazy and hot. Chewy and I sat on the lawn in front of the house, taking a break from the heat. We had parked our bikes in the front yard, ready to take off at any moment on our next adventure.

We looked down the street and saw several boys. Actually, I think I heard them first. They were laughing and joking around. They were taking turns hitting and pushing each other in order to attract our attention. Chewy and I watched as they made their way closer and closer to our house. Then, they began to snicker and I knew the boys were discussing Chewy and me. As they approached our house, the leader of the group called out to me.

"You guys new?" he asked, knowing full well we were.

"Yeah," I replied.

"Well, we have a rule in this neighborhood that we all share, and right now, I need to borrow your bike."

It was a direct challenge to me. I knew it, and he knew it. He waited for my response knowing that he might just as well have challenged me to a duel. I didn't answer but bounded from the steps and, in an instant, I stood nose-to-nose in front of this guy.

"You ain't taking my bike," I said.

"We'll just see about that," he dared me again. "You gonna stop me?"

If I had learned nothing else from Garfield, I learned that you don't give the other guy the chance to strike first. Before the boy knew what hit him, I was on him, pounding him with one fist and then the other. It surprised him so much that he never even had a chance to respond. He was beaten before he even began to fight. The challenge had been made and accepted. I gained respect, and a new regime was now in charge of our street.

"What's your name?" I asked the boy who I had just pounded.

"Erik," he said, wiping his nose with his arm.

"I'm Mike," I said, helping him up.

During the remainder of the summer, Erik and I became close friends, and life was generally uneventful.

"You'll still need to show Frankie who's the boss," Erik informed me during one of our many conversations that summer.

"Who's Frankie, and why is he so tough?" I asked.

"He just has clout, and he's not going to let you take his place as leader. You'll see when he gets home," Erik replied.

Where's he at this summer? I asked Erik.

His mom works for Goodyear and she makes some good money there. They went on vacation. I don't know where," Frankie said.

As fall drew closer, I began to mentally prepare myself for the contest that I knew was about to happen in order to maintain my status in the neighborhood.

As it turned out, Frankie was in my class at school, and on the first day, he threw out the red flag ready to take me down.

"Who's the new kid?" I heard him ask another student as he pointed over his shoulder at me with his thumb."

"Mike Minter," the boy said.

"He comes from the other side of town?" Frankie asked. I knew he was making a snide remark about money. I shifted in my seat and looked over at him staring at me.

"You think you can take me?" I asked softly.

"In a minute," he chided. "Just as soon as I get the chance."

I was getting angry now and ready to meet him head-on. "Where do you want to meet?" I asked.

"After school, down the block," he said.

"After school it is," I replied.

During the entire course of the day, Frankie commented about what he was going to do to me to the other students in the class, and I became more and more angry as the school day progressed. So, when the last bell sounded, I was more than ready for a fight.

We faced off with each other that day, but, as with Erik, I was determined not to give Frankie any advantage in this fight. There was no more trash talk. I just hit him as hard as I could and tackled him to the ground. I was on top of him, so mad that I was ready to make him see stars. I raised my arm with my fist balled up to make the most impact with, in this case, Frankie's face. Just as I was about to deliver the final blow, I looked down. Frankie was staring up at me and, in his eyes, I saw sheer terror. As I continued to look down, I really thought I could see all the way into his soul. It was the first time that I had ever looked into someone's eyes and had seen inside that person. I knew, in that instant, that Frankie was just a kid like me... trying to survive. Suddenly, a wave of compassion covered me, and all the anger and frustration that had built up during the day was gone.

I unballed my fist and got off him. Then, I held out my hand and said, "Look Frankie, I don't want to pound you." I think Frankie was as shocked as I was, but he responded to my offer and over the school year we became best friends.

I will never forget that moment, though, when I looked in Frankie's eyes and saw what he was thinking and feeling at that moment. Years later, I would do that on the football field, and the ability to see through someone's eyes and to his thoughts, would give me an advantage in the game. It allowed me to anticipate my opponents' moves so I could respond accordingly. With school having started, Chewy and I now turned our attentions to the fact that this school had its own football team, and we looked forward to tryouts. However, that initial elation quickly passed when we arrived for practice. It was obvious to us, from the beginning, that the coach and his assistants had already picked their starting team. Most of the boys had played for them the previous year, and I guess the coach knew what to expect from them. Also, the coach had two sons on the team. The only positions that were left were spots that would not see much playing time. I was so disappointed. I felt I had played well on the Boys Club team during the past year, and I couldn't see myself sitting on the bench for most of that season. Dejected and sullen, Chewy and I stood by the fence watching the practice.

As luck or fate would have it, one of the older boys on the team was the brother of my sister's girlfriend, Carmen Davenport. Walking home from school that day, Boo and Carmen just happened to be discussing the football team. Carmen was telling Boo what a great football player her brother was, and Boo was doing the same about us. That's when the discussion turned into an argument.

"The coach isn't going to let them play!" Carmen said.

"He's crazy, then," Boo retorted. "My brothers are better than any of them boys out there."

"I'll bet your brothers don't play," Carmen replied. "Everyone on the first team was there last year, and they all live in the same neighborhood."

At just that moment, Boo and Carmen passed the fence where Chewy and I stood talking. I guess Boo could see that Carmen was correct because we, in fact, were not practicing with the team. Boo went home immediately and found our stepdad who had just arrived from work. Boo related the conversation she'd had with Carmen and what she had seen when she passed us on her way home.

"Go get in the truck," Gene said to Boo. "Let's go find your brothers."

When they arrived at the school, my stepdad told us to get in the truck with Boo, and he went to find the coach.

"Why aren't you letting my boys play?" we heard Gene asked the coach. "You know you've got superstars on this team? My boys won the championship last year." That was almost true.

The coach made his excuses, and my stepdad ended the conversation by saying, "It's going be your loss that you won't play them."

He left the field and drove us straight to the Boys Club where we signed up for another year of football. He also made arrangements the Boys Club to pick Chewy and me up in their bus for practice, and to bring us back home again in the evening. That time was what I like to call a "God moment" in my life, because it was pivotal in how the rest of my elementary years in football would be spent. As I look back, I can now see the subtle role Gene played in the events of my early experiences, by keeping my desire to play football on track. Years later, he would again be the encouraging factor that led me back into football during my high school years. If he had not intervened, it is very possible that the spirit that drove my desire for the game could have easily faded. I can see, through him, how God sometimes works inconspicuously in lives, to bring about His desired results.

That year, I was introduced to a new coach, Jerome Connor, and he decided that my best position was as a running back. Under his direction, the team played with precision, working out plays that were far beyond the abilities of a normal team of boys only nine old. That year I scored 32 touchdowns. When I had the ball in my hands, I could see nothing but the end zone. Also, I was the biggest hitter and leading tackler on the team that year. With the leadership of Connor, our 18 year old coach, the Roosevelt Razorbacks went 8-0 to win the city championship. It was my first real taste of ultimate victory. Football had become my pulpit, my god and my sanctuary. Because of football, I was able to gain the respect of other people.

That was also the year that I was introduced to the concept that how you dress affects your attitude about yourself and of those around you. Coach Connor required all team members to dress appropriately before, during and after each game. Even if we were wearing hand-me-downs, each player wore a suit to the football field. The fans coming to the games noticed immediately. Whether we won or lost, we always looked like winners. That realization affected me deeply, and, even today, I am conscious of how I look to other people.

In the world of business, they call it "dress for success," and I have found it to be a valuable lesson. In fact, today, I try to instill this very same attitude in the young men I coach. I don't really care what they wear in their personal lives, although I like to see young men dressed appropriately. When it comes to "team," though, I believe a dress code exhibits the quality and characteristics of the team.

Also, that season, I learned how football changes your identity. Oklahomans are a melting pot of racial groups, and our team represented the vast majority of them. Although each team member brought his own culture and beliefs, we were no longer different when we put on our uniforms and went onto that field. There was no color or cultural barriers. We were united by one goal…to play football to the very best of our abilities. I learned, at this early age, what people, both young and old, can accomplish when they put aside their biases and unite together to accomplish an objective. Winning, of course, made the adventure even sweeter…and we won and won and won! During the remainder of my elementary years, Chewy and I continued to play on the Boys Club team, which was never defeated while we were on the team.

Now, winning, at any level, produces a celebrity status, and our consistent successes introduced me to the fact that football can change your life. People like winners! They cater to them. For instance, even at this early stage in my life, restaurants gave our team free meals. We were constantly acknowledged for our talents. It was an amazing reward for winning a championship, and I responded to that recognition with the determination that my future would definitely need to include football. With football, I had found a purpose and plan for my life.

From a personality standpoint, I consider myself very much like my mama. I called her "the quiet storm." Like her, I was a very reserved child. In school, I was never the one to stand out in the crowd. Nonetheless, when I was on the football field, I became a different person. Like my mama, when we found a passion in our lives, our personalities were on fire.

Another of my favorite pastimes was to watch wrestling on television. Every chance I got, my eyes were fixed on that black and white screen watching the men in the ring locked together in fierce combat. Only the commercials, advertising the upcoming Orange Bowl game, were as exciting as that wrestling match. It was December 1983, and the University of Nebraska was taking on the University of Miami at the Orange Bowl, in Florida, on January 1, 1984.

One particular player on the Nebraska team was my idol. Mike Rozier had just been announced as the Heisman trophy winner. He wore the number 30 jersey and I imitated everything he did. Years later, we met in person, and I told him about the effect he'd had on my life. Mike was overwhelmed that, as a 22-year-old athlete, he had that much influence over a nine-year-old boy who had never met him. Later, when I was drafted by the Carolina Panthers, I chose the number 30 jersey in honor of Mike Rozier and for the inspiration he had been to me.

"Chewy," I declared as we watched one of many game highlights featuring Rozier, "I'm going to play football for Nebraska one day, just like Mike Rozier."

"Uh huh," Chewy replied half-heartedly.

My brother's lukewarm response did not dissuade me, however. I had decided I was headed for Lincoln, Nebraska. It did not matter that I still had eight years to wait for that dream to come true. This was my choice, and this was what I was going to do.

Even then, I knew that playing football was not enough. Gaining admission to a school of that caliber would also take good grades. I decided, right then, that I would never again get a "C" on my report card, and I never did. I became an "A" student in elementary school, and throughout my entire high school years I never received less than a "B" grade in any subject.

My best subjects were math and science. One particular year my teacher offered a challenge to the class. The first person that could recite all the multiplication tables up to 100 would win a cash prize. As I sat listening to her relate the rules, I was determined that I would win that prize. Each day after school I laid on my bed, singing a multiplication song we had learned to help us remember. I began at 1 x 1 and sang each table until I came to one I did not know. I would learn that table, and then patiently begin again at 1 x 1 until I came to the next unknown quantity. I did this tenaciously each day until I was able to recite the entire table.

The next day I arrived at school proud and ready to claim my prize, which I did. In my mind it had belonged to be from the very first moment I heard about the contest. Yet, it wasn't really about the prize. I cannot even remember what I won. It was winning the competition that satisfied my soul so very much!

Looking back at that moment, I am in awe that, even at that early age, I was choosing a direction for my life. Today, when I am with my own four children, I am constantly reminded of this fact and eager to encourage them in whatever positive endeavors they choose. It is my belief that if you give children a proper focus, they will not drift from that path.

Don't misunderstand me. My life was far from ideal, but perhaps the dreams of a ten year old were not such a bad thing. At least they helped me endure the many stressful moments and events that surrounded my sisters, brother and me. In the middle of all this instability, I discovered, in football, what it felt like to be a winner, and I liked it!

This brings to mind an event that occurred when Chewy and I were playing football with some of the neighborhood boys. Now, Chewy was smaller than me, and there was one particular boy on the opposite team who singled him out to bully. It seemed that every time a play was run, this boy was determined to hit Chewy as hard as he could, knocking him flat on his back. Finally, I could stand it no longer.

I announced loudly and with as much anger in my voice as I could muster, "Whoever catches the next ball, I'm going to blast-just like you've been hitting on my brother."

The teams lined up and the ball was kicked. It flew high in the air and appeared to hang forever before making its descent. The ball whirled end over end. Then, with a thud, it hit the ground, bounced and rolled. To my surprise, no one rushed to take me up on my challenge. No one wanted to even touch the ball. In fact, once the ball had stopped, the other team slowly disbanded, leaving my team to stand there in amazement. I knew I would have followed through with my threat, but never got the chance to prove it because the opposing team just left the field and went home. At that moment, I realized perception can be a powerful tool, even when you're not the strongest or most forceful person on a team.

Life was good for a while. Chewy and I were on a winning football team, my grades were good in school, and I had gained the respect of certain neighborhood boys who got their confidence by bullying others who were weaker than themselves. I had just completed the sixth grade in school, but then my world changed…again.

Chapter 3

THE VALLEY OF DECISIONS

It is filled with forks in the road.
Each one guides us towards our destiny.

It was June 19, 1986. Chewy and I sat stiffly in our seats next to Mama, anxious to know the sentence that the judge was about to hand down to my stepdad. The sweltering heat of the courtroom made the anxiety of what was happening even more intense. I looked at Chewy as the bailiff instructed everyone to stand up.

Mama, Chewy and I had been there with Gene all day. Until this moment he had been out on bail. He was convinced that the judge was not going to send him to prison. He was going to beat the wrap.

"Wait until this is over," Gene said to Chewy and I as we stood in the hallway during one of the many courtroom breaks that day. "We're going to go Six Flags Over Texas," he said as he patted both of us on the shoulder. "You boys just be thinking about what you want to do when we get there."

Earlier that afternoon, Gene's case had been announced and he went forward with his attorney who pleaded with the court for leniency. This was the first time he had been arrested and he was sorry for the crime. The trial seemed to last for hours as the prosecutor and defense attorney haggled back and forth, trying to convince the jury that their case had more merit. Gene was nervous, but resolute.

As I sat impatiently waiting for it all to end, I was excited at the thought of going to Six Flags Over Texas. I had never been there and, to a 12-year-old boy, it was a magical place that transported you far beyond the reaches of normal life. Hurry up, I thought as we sat suspended in time. Let's get this over with.

"Order in the court," the bailiff finally announced as the sound of the gavel striking wood echoed through the courtroom.

"William Johnson," the judge's voice rang out, "you have been found guilty of selling a controlled substance. You will be incarcerated for a period not less than three nor more than 10 years.

For our whole family, it was a devastating moment. I watched sorrowfully as the only father I had ever known was led out of the courtroom in handcuffs. His sentence kept him in prison until I was in high school. As children, we had not been aware of his illegal activities. He never brought drugs to our house, nor did we ever see any drugs being sold to others. Thus, his arrest had been both a surprise and shock to our whole family. If Mama knew about his activities, she never indicated it to us. We left the courtroom that day, dejected and fearful of what our lives would be like now that our father would no longer have a part in them. At this time, I began to appreciate my mama's strength. No matter what life happened to throw at her, we were always her priority.

Eventually, Chewy and I did make it to Six Flags, but it was my sister, Boo, who finally took us there. I guess she saw the disappointment in our faces when we related the events of the trial. In the end, it was always Boo that came through to dredge away the mud that life sometimes threw at us.

When I think back to this time in Mama's life, I understand now how difficult it must have been. She was only in her 30's, but, by this time, she had been knocked down so many times. Yet, she always got up, dusted herself off and trudged onward. She was such a trooper. At 12-years-old, I know I could not possibly have understood how badly life can sometimes treat a person. Now, though, I realize how all her trials strengthened her. She could have given up, but she didn't. She always worked hard to make the lives of her children so much better by brushing aside the agonies that she endured.

Mama was a beautician. According to my sister, Boo, upon returning to

Lawton, after my dad's death, Mom had gone back to school to become a licensed practical nurse. Sometime during the training, however, she decided that her skills were better served as a beautician. One of Boo's vivid memories of that time occurred while my grandmother was still alive. While Mama attended school, we stayed with my grandmother. One day, Mama arrived at my grandmother's house to pick us up. When she came through the door, my grandmother and Boo received the shock of their lives. She had allowed herself to be used as a model for other students to practice their talents. Instead of the striking, long, black hair that we were accustomed to, she exhibited a short, red afro, which was a popular style of the '70s. Boo related that my grandmother was so mad at her for allowing them to ruin her beautiful hair that she slapped Mama hard across her face. Nevertheless, my mom wore that afro until it grew out once more. She was never afraid to take a chance, and I learned that same, daring attitude from her. If you don't step out sometimes, and try new things, you tend to lose out.

It was tough to see Mama go to work, though. I can remember sitting on the porch with Chewy, crying and begging her not to go. We hated it when she left. But Mama was a self-reliant and independent person, and there was never a time in our lives that she ever used government assistance to support her family, in spite of the fact that she had four children to support. I am extremely proud of her for that. I believe much of her toughness came from the circumstances of her life. That strength, which she passed on to each of her children, helped us to endure a great deal of adversity. As a family, we simply took life as it came to us and moved on.

The year that I left elementary school, and looked confidently towards Tomlinson Junior High School, was earmarked by several significant events in my life. The first was the imprisonment of my stepdad, who had supported both Chewy and me in our ambitions to play sports. The second occurred that summer, just before I entered seventh grade. I was riding my bicycle alone one afternoon and came to a sudden stop. I put my foot down hard to stabilize myself and heard a popping noise as my leg gave way and I fell to the ground. I repeatedly tried to get up, but my knee refused to support my body and I collapsed again and again. I had never experienced such an inability to control my movements, and it worried me. Eventually, I was able to make it home but my knee began to swell and was sore. In spite of this, I did not see a doctor. Money was too tight to spend on a doctor. Plus, I didn't think the injury was very bad. I figured I'd go home, put some ice on it and let it heal. Years later, when I was injured playing football for Nebraska, doctors told me that I had torn the cartilage in my knee.

When school began, I tried out for the football team but my knee was still sore and healing. The coaches did not allow me to play very much, and it was difficult for me to watch other players while I sat on the bench. Perhaps if my knee had not been injured, I would have been able to compete to my abilities and the coaches would have used my talents more. Regardless, I spent most of that season on the bench, losing my enthusiasm to play football at all.

I did not even try out for the football team in the eighth grade. That year, basketball became my sport of choice. Tomlinson had won the championship in basketball the previous year, and the football team was, in my opinion, average. We had moved from Country Club into the area of Lawton known as Lawton View. Comparing Lawton View to the other areas of town in which we had lived was like comparing apples to oranges. When we lived on Washington Street, the area was rundown and definitely dominated by the poor economies of those that lived there. Then we moved up to the Country Club area, a middle-class black community. The schools were better. It was far away from the drug activities carried out on "the hill," and life, in general, was pleasant.

After Gene's staggering exit from our family, I guess Mama couldn't afford the luxury of living in such a high rent district. Washington Street was poor, but Lawton View was another rung lower on the ladder. If a town of about 70,000 could have an "inner city," the Lawton View district was it. It was so bad that, initially, Chewy and I were afraid to go to the local multipurpose center, where the swimming pool was located. We finally met a boy from the neighborhood who knew I played football and he became our intermediary to introduce us safely into the local culture.

This was the year that I met my best friend, Thaddeous Turner. We had known of each other through school, but we had never hung out together. He was tall and lanky, and played on the basketball team. I also went out for basketball that year and ended up playing point guard. That year, Tomlinson won the basketball championship once again. Both of us were good at sports, and we both wanted good grades in school. We enjoyed many of the same activities so, naturally, we became best friends. From that time on, Thad was always at our house sleeping over or we were at his. Thad, Chewy and I were like the Three Musketeers, always together doing something. Thad became my second brother and remains so today.

My knee had completely healed by the time I began the ninth grade, so I decided to try out for football and, once again, I found myself playing at running back. We barely missed winning the championship, finishing the year at 9-1. Football had become fun once more.

Thad did not play football, only basketball, but as soon as football season was over, Thad, Chewy and I were together again on the basketball court, playing as if basketball was king. That year, Tomlinson had a 17-1 season and I decided that basketball was the sport I would stay with for the next school year. At least for the time being, my enthusiasm for playing on the University of Nebraska football team had faded.

During this period of my life, my stepfather re-entered our family. After all the years of learning to live without him, he showed up at our door one day as if he had never been gone. It was a difficult adjustment for me. Everything was different now and it would never be the same again. However, just as he had done when I was eight years old, he played a very influential part in my life.

I had decided not to play football in 10th grade. When the time came for tryouts, I didn't go. The football coach at Lawton High School, Pat Hunt, called me over and over again. He tried his best to encourage me to try out for the team, but I was indecisive and wasn't really sure if I wanted to play. Finally, I stopped answering the phone because I didn't want to talk to him.

Thad and Chewy kept urging me to try out and my stepdad said to me, "Mike, you really ought to try out for the team. You are a natural football player, son, and it would be a shame for you not to play. Now that you're in high school, scouts will be coming to look at you. Besides, you're too short to play basketball in college. Football can offer you more opportunities than you can imagine. Think about it. Think about what you want to do with your life. Football is one of the ways you can get to where you want to go."

I knew that everyone was right about the opportunities that football offered, so I reluctantly joined the team that year. I returned to my first love and slowly the anticipation of playing professional football surfaced once more. I might have been sidetracked for a little while, but now, my dream was back and I owed it to myself to see it through. I started at cornerback and running back. It was a decision that I would never regret. But secretly, I was still scared that I was too small to play on a high school football team. Elementary and junior high teams were one thing, but those high school guys hit hard...really, really hard. The same fear that tried so hard to influence my life would resurface again in the future when I was making my choice about where I would play college football.

The next few years were a whirlwind of activity. Choosing to play football again did not mean I had given up basketball. For the remainder of my high school years I played on both teams. Since the football season overlapped basketball, a lot of flexibility was required by both coaches. Coach Wade, the basketball coach, was very lenient with Chewy and me regarding practices, and even the initial games of the season.

By the 11th grade, colleges start to get serious about signing prospective players up for their teams. Once again, my statement to Chewy came back. I had always wanted to go to Nebraska and had made no secret of it. So it is not without wincing that I remember the day the high school head football coach, Derald Ahschlager, called me into his office.

"Mike," he said, "I know you're looking forward to being picked by Nebraska, but I'm afraid you just aren't fast enough or big enough to play with those boys. I think you need to consider the possibility of signing with a smaller school. You would still get to play on a scholarship."

Speechless, I looked at him with amazement. In all my years of playing football on winning teams, I had never once considered the fact that I might not be chosen by Nebraska, should I decide to go there. At that moment I was forced to make a decision that I would never regret. I could believe someone else's negative perspective, or make a choice to try to take his observations and let them be a guide, to help me work for what I wanted to achieve. It opened my eyes to the fact that, in order to make myself an attractive prospect, I needed to excel in every way during the next two seasons. I lifted weights and worked out constantly. During my junior year I played harder than ever before. I never let up and I made sure that I was playing football to the best of my abilities. I was determined that if I was rejected, it would not be due to my speed or size.

My senior year of high school began with the traditional visit to the guidance counselor in preparation for college.

"What subjects are you interested in studying in college, Mike?" she asked.

I looked around the small and somewhat cluttered room that defined most guidance counselors, not knowing exactly what my response should be. Until that moment, I hadn't really considered what I would study in college. In high school they always tell you what you need to take in a college prep program. College was different, and I was just beginning to understand how different.

"I'm not sure," I said.

"Well," she persisted, "what classes do you like here at Lawton?"

"I like math," I said.

The counselor, a somewhat petite woman who had always been very nice to me, began listing several courses of study that would utilize my mathematical skills. After a few moments, I interrupted.

"What fields of study make a lot of money?" I asked, suddenly considering the possibility that I just might have to support myself with an occupation other than football.

She looked at me as if she was surprised by the question.

"Engineering makes a lot of money," she replied. "You have good grades in math so you shouldn't have trouble with those courses."

I nodded, considering the possibility.

"Which field of engineering makes the most money?" I asked, trying to narrow down my options.

"Mechanical engineering," she said.

"Then sign me up for mechanical engineering," I said.

I left her office confident of my choice. My reasoning was simple. If football did not prove to be the road to financial success, then mechanical engineering would have to fill in the gap.

During football tryouts that year, all my conditioning paid off. I ran the 40-yard dash in 4.5 seconds-the fastest time on the team. I was anxious to see the coach's reaction, since he had made that comment to me during the past year about not being fast enough to play for Nebraska. He was impressed but decided to change me from running back to slot receiver or wing guy. I was not at all happy with that decision.

That year the University of Miami was considered one of the top college teams. They played a spread offense, which put only one running back in the backfield as opposed to the two running backs in the typical pro-set of the day. So Coach Ahlschlager decided he was going to use that same offense for Lawton, and he wanted to use another player in that running back position. This guy fit the mold of what the coach wanted. He was big and I was small.

Usually, I was a quiet kid who didn't say much. I just took whatever came my way and tried to make the best of it. But, this time, I was so mad that I began asking myself, what do I do? I knew I was never going to be happy playing as a slot receiver. I was a running back and that's the position that I wanted to play.

Chewy played as a receiver, too. That night we were talking and I finally said, "Chewy I don't want to play receiver. I'm a running back and that's where I want to be.

"You shouldn't be there. You should be the running back," Chewy agreed.

"But what should I do?" I asked.

"I don't know," Chewy sighed.

"I'm just going to have to go talk to him," I finally said.

I didn't sleep at all that night because I was still so mad. I finally came to the conclusion that I would have to tell the coach that I wasn't a receiver and he needed to play me as a running back. If he didn't, I decided I would go to another school where I could play running back. I tossed and turned all night. I'd close my eyes and try to go to sleep, but just as I was about to drift off, I remembered that the next day might end my football career at Lawton High School. My eyes would pop open and I would find myself once again staring at the wall in my dark bedroom. Five minutes seemed more like an hour, and the night just seemed to go on and on with no end to it. Meanwhile, my mind kept rehearsing what I was going to say to the coach. I must have played out just about every conceivable scenario before I realized that morning had finally arrived. I was mad, but I was scared too. The thought of facing the coach and offering an ultimatum terrified me.

That morning we rode the bus to school as usual. As we got off the bus and were walking down the school hallway, I was once again playing the scene over and over in my mind. What I was going to say to Coach? I can't even count how many ways I went through the conversation in my mind. With each variation, I got more and more scared about what was going to happen. Then I looked down the hall and there he was coming towards us.

As I look back, it was as if God had set up the whole situation for me to see him, because I had never before seen the coach walking through the halls. At that instant I said to myself, here comes the moment!

As Coach approached us, I stopped him. The words rushed out of my mouth. "Coach, I don't want to play receiver because I'm not a receiver. I'm a running back and I need to play running back, and that's what I'm going to play or I'm going to go to another school." I continued, "This is not right. I see what you're trying to do, but I don't agree with it."

Coach didn't really say anything for a moment. I think he was totally caught off guard because I was usually such a quiet kid. It really surprised him that I would come out and say what I did. I think this was the first time I had ever stood up to a coach. But from that day on he put me back as running back. I'm not sure what changed his mind. Maybe it was the intensity I had. I don't know, but in that moment everything changed. It changed my football season and it changed the season for the whole team. That year I was the leading rusher in the state of Oklahoma with 1,589 rushing yards. I scored 21 touchdowns and was chosen as all-state in Oklahoma.

One of our games was against Norman Oklahoma High School. The day before the game, the coach told me that the University of Nebraska coaches were coming down to see me and another player on the team-Daryl Gardener. We were really excited when we got the news that they would be coming the next night. Daryl and I had become close football buddies during the senior season, as the recruiters started looking at both of us for college teams. We decided between ourselves that we were going to go to Nebraska together to play football.

Coaches from Nebraska were actually coming to see us! I was so fired up I couldn't sleep. All I could do was think about it. I was determined to run the ball so hard that I literally ran over people.

From the opening kickoff, no one could stop me from making plays all over the field. I could swear that I felt electricity running through every muscle in my body. I was on fire and I knew it. In high school, I played both offense and defense, although I realized that I would probably have to concentrate on defense for the Nebraska team. That night I played safety on defense and I was hitting people so hard that I had about two or three "knock 'em into the cheap seats" hits. I desperately wanted to prove to those Nebraska coaches that I could play big-time college football and by the time the game had ended, I had made about 10 to 12 tackles and more than 100 yards running. I was also satisfied that I had showed power in some of my runs.

I remember that every time I did something notable, I was thinking, I wonder, did they see that? I wonder what they thought of that. I wonder if they liked that. I was used to scoring when I played offense, so I was a bit disappointed when I didn't score that night. But I had a great defensive game. We won 14-0.

Afterwards, Coach Ahlschlager came to see Daryl and me.

"They were pretty impressed with you both," he said. "They liked what they saw and want to come to Lawton and talk to you guys."

That year the Lawton High School football team went all the way to the semi-finals of the championship game. During the finals, I had the flu and was so sick, but I played anyway. If I hadn't been sick I believe we would have won. I played the first half and ran about 60 yards for a touchdown, but I kept throwing up and couldn't play the last half of the game. We ended up losing 21-

7. Our high school season was almost over, and my high school career completed. Unlike my fears when it came to jumping to high school-level football, I was now confident and ready to take the next step…college football…and at the University of Nebraska, I hoped.

I remember the first call I got from Tom Osborne, head football coach at the University of Nebraska.

"How ya doing, Michael?" Coach said to me over the telephone. His voice was so cool and calm and he talked slowly.

"I just wanted you to know that we're interested in you coming to Nebraska. We like what we see in you and you're a good student. You take school very well and we have a great engineering program. I look forward to coming to see you. How would you like for us to come down and make a visit at your house?"

Wow, I'm thinking. I can't believe I'm talking to Coach Osborne and he's going to come and see me!

It was January, and football season had ended and basketball had begun. During one game we were playing Eisenhower High School, which was our across-town rival. Coach Osborne came down along with one of his assistant coaches, Milt Tenopir, who had been scouting me throughout the football season. Both men were in the stands, watching me play basketball. The game went into triple overtime, and Osborne and Tenopir left early. When I got home, I saw they were there waiting for me. I was still outside and I remember saying to Chewy, "This is it. Tom Osborne is in my house right now to offer me a scholarship."

Tom Osborne had been the head coach of the Cornhuskers football team since 1973 and he was here to see me! During his 25 seasons as head coach, he led Nebraska's football team to 255 wins, 49 losses and three ties. This impressive record won him the Home Depot Coach of the Year Award in 1999, and he was recognized as coach of the decade. He left coaching in the 1998 season to run for the U.S. Congress and served six years as a representative from Nebraska's third congressional district. In 2007 he was awarded the Paul "Bear" Bryant Lifetime Achievement Award and, in October of that same year, he returned to the University of Nebraska as athletic director.

That night, though, was like a dream, almost an out-of-body experience for me, like when things happen that just don't seem real.

Coach Osborne was already a giant in my mind, but when he stood up to greet me, it surprised me how tall he really was. I can still remember walking in and smiling at him as he shook my hand. I was trying so hard to keep it together. In my mind I wanted to run around the house and shout, or run outside and just fall down on the grass. I was so happy and excited. Mama was there with an uncle and my sisters. Chewy was with me. Suddenly, I realized this wasn't just my dream coming true. This was their dream also. I could barely contain my emotions as we all sat down and listened as Coach Osborne started talking about the university and what a great place it was. Then he got to the point of his visit.

"Michael, we want to offer you a scholarship. Do you want to come to Nebraska?"

There was a hush in the room as he waited for my answer, but in my mind I was screaming, what a crazy thing to ask me. Of course I want to go. Take me with you tonight. I want to go so much!

"Thank you Coach Osborne," I replied as calmly as possible. "I would like very much to go to Nebraska next year."

My answer invoked a shout from Mama and she and my sister, Boo, were crying and laughing at the same time. It was a sharp contrast to the quiet in the room only moments before.

Then Coach Osborne started reassuring Mama.

"You don't need to worry about Mike. I'll take good care of him."

Coach Osborne had brought with him so much hope, and it filled the room to overflowing. It was the fulfillment of so many dreams and the beginning of a new milestone in my life.

A week later I went on a recruiting trip to Nebraska. It was the first time I had ever been away from home and the first time I had ever flown on an airplane. The coaches had sent a little four-seat plane to pick me up after a basketball game. All I could think about that night was what it was going to be like getting on that plane. I was nervous, but I'm the type of person that, when there's something new, I might be nervous but I still want to try it. I love to try new things and this was certainly a new adventure for me. As the plane lifted from the runway, I thought, I'm one step closer to my dream. It began with a television commercial for the Orange Bowl…it was a dream that would ultimately take me places I had only imagined.

During the short flight to Lincoln, I looked out the window of the plane into the blackness of the night. I could hear the low whirring of the plane's single engine and felt relieved that my first flying experience was not so frightening after all. However, sitting there alone in the plane, I felt that I was also looking into my unknown future, and it was far more frightening than the thought of flying had ever been to me.

When we landed, reality set in. My first reaction when I stepped off that plane was, man, what did I get myself into? Now, understand that, to this day, I swear that Nebraska is so flat you can see from one side of the state to the other. As a result, there's nothing to stop the wind, and this was definitely a cold wind, and I didn't even have a coat!

I was immediately shocked to find that the temperature there was nine degrees Fahrenheit, and I'm standing there with no coat. It never occurred to me to bring one because Lawton's temperature is very mild. A temperature of 30 degrees was cold to me, so this was triple cold!

Will Shields, a member of the Nebraska football team, was sent to meet me at the airport. Daryl had driven to Lincoln and met us on campus. Will had been assigned to show us around and take us to our hotel room. He was an offensive guard for Nebraska from 1989 to 1992. This was his final year, and he had already been selected as an All-American and won the Outland Trophy award. In 1993, he was picked in the third round of the NFL draft and went on to play his entire professional career with the Kansas City Chiefs. He had also played football at Lawton High School. Although he was three years older than me, I still remembered him from high school.

While we were being shown the campus, I kept thinking to myself, this is nuts. We're out here in the middle of nowhere and it's cold! I don't want to go to a place this cold! After all the years of yearning to go here, now I wasn't so sure it was what I wanted.

When we got back to Lawton, however, Daryl and I committed to go to Nebraska and I thought everything was set. Then, about a week later, Daryl called me on the telephone.

"What's up, man?" I asked.

"I've got to tell you something. I've changed my mind about going to Nebraska. I'm going to Baylor instead," Daryl informed me.

"What?" I exclaimed. "Baylor? What are you talking about? We're going to Nebraska!"

"No, man, Baylor is the place, man," he replied. "I'm telling you that Baylor was so good and so much fun when I went on a recruiting trip. It's close to home and, man I'm telling you that it's where we need to go."

"You talked to them about me?" I asked.

"Yeah, and they want you to come, too."

"Man, tell them to call me and I'll go to Texas and visit," I sighed. "I guess we're going to go to Baylor."

The Baylor coaches called me that very night to set up the plane trip and I flew there the next night. But, when I arrived, I just didn't feel it. The same excitement that Daryl had conveyed over the phone didn't come across to me. The dorms were nice and they had nice things to say about the university that were very appealing, but I just didn't feel the connection. I didn't feel like this was where I was supposed to be.

Then Baylor offered me a scholarship and fear began to set in. It began to drive me because, even though I didn't feel a connection to Baylor, I didn't want to go somewhere by myself. I kept thinking, man, I don't want to go all the way to Nebraska by myself. Daryl and I were going to have each other to hang out with in Nebraska while we learned about college life and played football together. Now I'd be going alone and it scared me to think about it. My frustration grew as once again the words rang out in my head. What should I do?

Wherever I was going to school had to be decided immediately because it was February, and the next day was signing day. That night was one of the most terrifying nights I can remember in my life. I was awake the entire night, tossing and turning. My mind played out every possibility. Should I go with Daryl? Should I follow my dream? I wanted desperately to go to Nebraska, but then Daryl wanted me to go with him to Baylor. If I went to Nebraska, I would be on my own, totally by myself. It was an awesome decision for an 18-year-old boy who had never lived away from home before now. In my mind I cried out, God, what should I do?

The next day I arrived at school with the two Fed-Ex packets. Each one contained an unsigned agreement for each of the two schools. Now, Coach Ahlschlager knew I had visited Baylor. He was a Nebraska guy and he loved Nebraska. The media had all arrived at the school for a big press conference to announce the schools that Daryl and I would be attending. We were in the coach's office waiting when Coach asked Daryl to leave the room for a minute. At that point I was still undecided about what choice I would make.

"Mike, are you going to let the opportunity to go to Nebraska go away?" He looked directly at me. "You've always wanted to go there. So now it's up to you to decide what you want to do."

I sat there in limbo, not knowing what to say. Then suddenly, I just blurted it out, "Nebraska. I'm going to Nebraska." I was shocked that out of my mouth came words I wasn't even thinking.

Coach Ahlschlager called everyone into the room and said to the press, "I'm so thankful to have two young men on my football team that are going on to play college football. Daryl Gardener is going to Baylor and Mike Minter is going to the University of Nebraska."

Daryl Gardener went to Baylor and was later drafted as a first round pick for the Miami Dolphins in 1996. He also played for the Washington Redskins and retired from the Denver Broncos in 2004.

The moment that led up to that final decision of where to go to college, was another turning point in my life. All the agony that I had experienced the day before was gone. I signed the contract to go the University of Nebraska and from that moment on, I was ready to go.

When I look back over my life, I see how fear can be such a master if you allow it to be. It can stop people from living out their dreams. That's why I'm such an advocate of telling people that you don't stop because of fear. Fear is not from God. You have to overcome it. You have to keep going. You've got to step through it. When you step through it and you're on the other side, you'll be able to look back and say, "Man, I'm glad I kept going."

Along with that lesson that day, I also learned that you need to be patient. God will answer your prayers. Don't rush and don't hurry. It doesn't matter if you are down to the last second. I was down to the last second. God will give you direction just as He gave me direction. At the very point I had to announce my decision, He gave me the words "Nebraska. I'm going to Nebraska."

Chapter 4

NEBRASKA, HERE I COME

Not everything always goes quite as planned
so be prepared for the detours.

The decision was made and the rest of the school year was spent getting ready to leave for college after graduation. Being an 18-year-old-guy who had never lived away from home before, I didn't even know what I needed to take with me when I left for college. My sister Boo was a great help. She is almost seven years older then me so she took things under control and shopped for all the dorm supplies I would need, such as bedding, towels, etc.

The night before I was to leave, I was so excited that I couldn't sleep a wink. I had made arrangements to ride to Nebraska with a guy named Ben Rutz. He was quarterback for a high school in Oklahoma City that Lawton had actually competed against, but the two of us never met until after the season was over. Both of us were named All-American scholar athletes and All-State (Oklahoma) and we met at those games. Also, we each received a $1,000 scholarship from Oklahoma and met again when we arrived at Edmond, Oklahoma to receive the award. Over this period of time we became friends because we were both going to Nebraska to play football. The year was 1992, and Ben and I left Oklahoma with the highest of expectations for our mutual successes.

Ben's career in football eventually ended up as what some sports reporters call "snake bit." He went to Nebraska with the intention of winning the starting quarterback job that year, but lost his bid to Tommie Frazier, a young quarterback from Bradenton, Florida. His goal to skip his 1992 redshirt (freshman) year and go straight to eligibility was detoured.

In spite of his abilities, Ben's luck went from bad to worse that year. He ended up splitting time with Tommie on the first-team offense during the 1993 spring drills, but tore his ACL (anterior cruciate ligament) during practice. By fall he was ready to play again but by then Tommie had won the job. Just after the 1993 season began, Ben transferred, finally ending up with the Kansas University "Jayhawks."

In 1994 and 1995, Tommie led Nebraska to back-to-back national championships and ended his career with a Big Eight record of 33-3. In 1996, his number 15 jersey was retired by Nebraska, while, in 2006, an ESPN.com poll voted the 1995 Nebraska team "the best college team of all time." Ironically, Ben Rutz eventually won the starting quarterback position for the Kansas City Jay Hawks, but neither he nor Tommie Frazier went on to play professional sports.

I was excited when I arrived at school and I got my dorm assignment. In Lawton we had Cameron University, but those dorms were not nearly as impressive as the ones at the University of Nebraska. I didn't have a roommate and was happy about that. I thought, wow! This is great! It's just me! But I soon found out that it was more difficult than I had anticipated. Daryl had gone to Baylor and I was on campus by myself, without my family or the friend I had depended on to get me through this time of initiation into college life. The dorms were nice, but cold and impersonal. I was used to being around a lot of people I knew and loved. I began to miss the warmth of a home atmosphere immediately. In fact, I craved it.

I was also concerned that this was my redshirt year in football. I was constantly worried, along with the other redshirts, whether the coaches liked me or not. During this year I did not play in an actual game. Redshirts only practiced with the team. However, I knew that if the coaches liked what they saw in practice, I would officially be part of the team the next season. Nevertheless, it ate at me to only be a spectator on Saturdays. Fortunately, Will Shields helped me to deal with that frustration.

Will was always saying to me, "Mike, everybody goes through this. Everybody's got to do this. The coaches like what you're doing and want you to be here. They really like what they see."

That conversation was what kept me going because I knew what the other freshmen didn't know, that the coaches liked me. I have Will to thank for getting me through that first year. When I got to college I was wide open. I was in everything. A bunch of us freshmen would get together and go out on the town, trying to find something to do. I never drank or did drugs or anything like that-because football was king-but I loved having fun. I had to learn, though, to be responsible for the freedom I had and how I used my time. I needed to learn to deal with that freedom. College was so different from high school. If I wasn't in class, I wasn't marked tardy or absent. I just had to make sure that I was at football practice when it started.

One Friday night, early in the fall of my redshirt freshman year, my buddies and I ended up at a community dance. That night I was scouting the ladies. Here I was, a dude with a wad of money in his pocket from my Pell Grant, trying to find a girlfriend, or at least someone to talk to.

I looked across the room full of people, dancing or clustered together talking and I saw this beautiful girl with curly, long, blond hair. I said to myself, man, I have got to talk to her. So I made my way slowly to where she was standing and asked for her name.

"Kim Rose," she answered.

I asked her if she wanted to dance. She was kind of shy but she said, "Yes." We danced for a minute and tried to talk, but the noise of the music coupled with the sounds of everyone trying to talk above it, made it difficult to hear each other. "Let's go outside," I said.

Outside we exchanged the general information usually given when two people meet each other for the first time. Of course, I was trying my best to be cool. Kim, on the other hand, was trying her best to be nonchalant. Finally, I asked, "Mind if I call you later?" She agreed. My next move was trying to look sharp to this beautiful chick. I pulled out a wad of cash, peeled off a $20 bill, and wrote her name and telephone number on it.

"I'll give you a call," I said as we went back inside. With nothing more to say for the moment, she went back to her friends and I went to mine.

At that time, Kim never realized her number was one of about 10 names and numbers I acquired that night, all in the same manner. Each one was carefully written for the effect they produced, on a $20 bill. Or, maybe she did know of my deception because, the next day I dialed her number and her mom answered.

"Is Kim there? I asked.

"No," she replied, "She's not here right now."

For some reason, I had the impression that I was being put off. "Well, tell her that Mike Minter called and I'll call her later," I said.

"Okay," her mom said.

I looked at my list of numbers, crossed her name off and went on to the next one.

During the month of November of that first semester, another football teammate, Clinton Childs, came to me and said, "Mike I've got somebody you need to meet. I think you two would be a good couple."

So I said, "Okay, cool," thinking I was about to meet another new girl.

I went over to Clinton's dorm room to meet this girl he thought was so right for me. I had no idea until she walked in that it was the same girl I had met at the dance months before. She arrived and, to my surprise, it was Kim, still quiet and shy, with that long curly blond hair. She was so beautiful, it took my breath away. She was the very first white girl I had ever been involved with that way. Until then, I always believed that you stay on your side and let them stay on theirs. We talked for a while. Then, all of a sudden, I realized that I really liked her. Now, I'm a very straightforward person when I'm talking to people. So, as I was walking her back to her car, I just came right out and said to Kim, "Do you have a boyfriend?"

"No," she said.

"Maybe I should be your boyfriend. What do you think about that?" I continued.

"Well, I don't know about that," she replied.

"You think about it and let me know later, okay?" I teased.

We began by just talking on the telephone. Then I went to her house and met her mom, Debbie. It was the first time I had ever been around white people like that. Usually my exposure was just football players and schoolmates, but her family was so "cool," it shocked me. Before I met them, I saw white people with a stigma because I thought that they just didn't get black folks. My people all felt that white people could never relate to the pain that came out of the slavery that the blacks were forced to endure. Not only were white people unable to relate to the depth of that pain, they just plain didn't care. In their minds, what happened more than 100 years before was past history and needed to be forgotten. I grew up in that environment. Now, I was living in a place that was 90 percent white folks, so I was a little nervous when I met her family. I knew I could hold a conversation with anyone, though, so I wasn't worried about that part of it.

From our first meeting, Debbie Rose was cool and laid back. I really liked her and the way she treated me with such respect and love. I wondered what her dad, Dan, was like, but it was sometime later before we met.

Kim and I were dating steadily, our relationship growing more serious as first semester drew to an end. She would pick me up at the stadium after practice and I would go to her house. Then I came to a point where I liked it better at her house than I did at the dorm. Since I still wasn't playing regular season football, I had plenty of free time.

November 14, 1992 was one of the last football games of my redshirt season and Nebraska was playing Iowa State. The Rose family was traveling to Ames, Iowa to watch the game and I was invited to come. It was the first time I had the opportunity to meet Kim's dad, Dan. As I remember, though, the only thing I said to him was "hello."

I spent the whole trip sitting in the back seat of the car with my headphones on, listening to my music and rapping out loud along with it. The music was the kind that most parents don't want their kids to hear. I never cussed, but I loved listening to rap music, which had a lot of foul language in it. It just resonated with what I had gone through in my life and I identified with it. Back then, it just made sense to me.

Nebraska lost that game to Iowa, 19-10. I was so mad that, on the way back, I didn't say anything. We did eventually end up with a 9-3 record that season, but I hated that we lost that particular game. Plus, I was anxious for my redshirt year to end so I could be out on that field myself.

In any event, what Kim's dad saw when he first met me didn't make a very good first impression. His perception was that I was an angry guy who didn't say much, but loved rap music. Years later, he told me that his first impression had been, man, what is wrong with this kid? Kim, you better stay away from him!

By now, I was really starting to feel deeply about Kim. I was even thinking that this is the girl I would like to marry. I've always been a family-oriented person, and I preferred one solid relationship to focus on along with football. This relationship with Kim was beginning to fit into that category for me. I was never into the typical college lifestyle habit of dating lots of girls, with no serious ties.

Christmas break arrived, but Ben Rutz wanted to stay in Lincoln for an additional week to visit with friends. Since he was my ride, I needed to find a place to stay since the dorms were closed. Kim's family extended an invitation to stay with them. Their home had a finished basement where one of Kim's younger sisters, Melissa, had her bedroom. She moved upstairs and I stayed in her room during that week. I was not used to houses that had basements. In Oklahoma, houses were traditionally built on a concrete slab. Sleeping in a room underground was a new experience for me, but it gave me additional time with Kim, and it also enabled me to spend time getting to know her family. It was the first time I was able to be in an intimate situation with people from a different race. The more time I spent with them, the more I came to feel they were "cool" people just like the people I had known all my life.

I think that was when I began to see people as individuals, regardless of skin color, or where they came from, or what they'd done. It taught me a lesson I have never forgotten. You can't judge someone because of what you think, or what you've read, or the past history of a people. Yes, there are bad white people, but there are bad people in every race. From that point on, my thinking was totally redirected to judging people on their own individual merits.

That week was so great for me. I was just a redshirt freshman. I wasn't a star. Nobody knew who I was. Nevertheless, the Rose family took me into their home and treated me like their own family. I didn't spend Christmas with them, but we actually had a Christmas celebration before I left for home. They got me some presents and I sat there thinking, this is cool.

During my time at home that December, I called Kim all the time to find out what she was doing. I had begun acting like a "loopy" teenager who was falling in love. My mom noticed and so did my sister Boo. I finally decided I would tell them why.

"I have a girlfriend in Nebraska, I said to them nonchalantly, "and I really like her." Then the words just came out of my mouth. "She's white."

"What? What you talking about?" Boo asked. My sister had grown up during the 1970s, so her reaction to my news was not received very well.

Then mom said, "You're crazy, boy! You better get your butt in gear and quit acting."

I've always been a person that understood the depths of slavery and I understood the depths of hurt that the black people felt, and I attributed much of that pain to white people…that is, until I met Kim and her family. When I met them, it opened my eyes to a whole new world. Is that pain significant? Absolutely! But you can't judge everyone by that pain. That's what I tried to tell them, as I was explaining to them my relationship with Kim.

I remember telling my best friend Thad Turner about Kim. His reaction was the same as Mom's and Boo's. "What you talking about? She's a white girl! You know we don't mess around with that," he said.

"Man," I said. "I know, but she's different. I'm telling you, she's different. When you meet her, you'll see what I'm saying. She's not the typical white girl that you're thinking about. She understands," I said, pleading my case to Thad.

"I've got to see for myself. I've got to meet her, man," Thad replied.

"You'll see when you meet her," I said.

I returned to school in January. In the spring, Mama and Boo traveled to Nebraska to watch me play in a redshirt game. While they were in Lincoln, I was able to introduce them to Kim, her parents and her two younger sisters, Cortney and Melissa.

Mama finally said, "Okay, I like them."

However, my sister, Boo, was still adamant. "Uh uh! You need to quit going over there so much and get back to the dorm! What are you doing?" I realize now that much of Boo's apprehension revolved around the fear that I was about to do something that would jeopardize everything I had worked so hard to achieve. She knew how much she had given up by not attending college when she had the opportunity, and she did not intend to let me fall into the same trap.

I said, "Boo, it's all right. They're cool. They're taking care of your brother up here."

"I don't care," Boo said. "You get back to that dorm and focus on school and football!"

"All right, Boo, okay," I said to calm her fears.

But, inside, I was saying to myself, seriously, I get to keep my scholarship next year, these are great people, and I'm in love with their daughter. Man, there is no way I'm going to stay away from Kim. This is Heaven!

I believe that if I hadn't met Kim's family, my life would not have turned out the way it did. I think they were God sent from Heaven. He used them to open my eyes about people and to give me love when I needed it, at a time when I felt so vulnerable. They just let me be me. Sure, I made mistakes, but they let me grow and supported me by becoming my family away from home. It was on this foundation that my relationship with Kim was built.

In the summer of 1993, before football camp began that year, Kim and I traveled back to Lawton together. On the way, we stopped by Thad's house so I could introduce her. Thad had married his high school sweetheart, Tonya, and already had a family to support. After meeting Kim, Thad admitted to me that I was right about her.

Before we arrived in Lawton, I had to prep Kim about our reception. I said to her, "First of all, you've never seen anything like my people. Second, you've got to understand that they don't like white people, so it's going to be tough. Mama is going to tell you like it is, so you've got to take it for what it's worth and keep rolling. You've got to have thick skin."

I had Kim so scared. She was nervous when we got there, but she was fine. Everyone liked her, except Boo. My sister still wouldn't change her mind. She just refused to move forward.

"No! No! No!" Boo said to me while we were there visiting.

"This is what I'm going to do," I tried to explain to her. But she still said "No!" She was nice to Kim, but I know my sister and she didn't like our being together at all.

On September 4, 1993, Nebraska took on North Texas, and I started in my first regular game for the Cornhuskers as a safety. Man, I was fired up. The rush of adrenalin I felt that day made my skin tingle from the inside out. Every hair on my body was standing at attention. I felt beads of sweat forming on my forehead. I was ready, and I wanted to hit somebody, anybody…friend or foe. I had waited my whole life for this moment and, as I stood on the field that day, I saw my future before me.

During that game the coaches switched me off with another guy. I played two series of downs, then he came in and played two series. I knew that the coaches were sizing each of us up to decide which was the best choice was for this safety position. I was determined to make that choice easy for them. Nebraska devastated North Texas 76-14. In fact, the whole season 1993 was a monumental one in my life. Ultimately, we went 11-0 in the regular season, even beating one of our biggest rivals, the University of Oklahoma, 21-7.

On January 1, 1994, we played Florida State in the championship game at the Orange Bowl in Miami, Florida. That had been Nebraska's best season since 1983, the year Chewy and I sat glued to the television watching Mike Rozier. In that game, Nebraska had lost 31-30 in a well-fought championship to the University of Miami.

Nebraska was ranked No.2 in 1993 and we anticipated the challenge of playing the No. 1 one ranked team, Florida State. The first quarter was scoreless, mainly due to great defense on the part of both teams. Then, into the second quarter, Scott Bentley kicked a 33-yard field goal for FSU to put the Seminoles on the scoreboard with a 3 point lead. Tommie Frazier answered back for us with a 34-yard touchdown pass to wide receiver, Reggie Baul. This gave Nebraska a 7-3 lead. With only 29 seconds left in the half, Florida State kicked a 25-yard field goal to make the score 7-6 at halftime. In the third quarter, FSU'S William Floyd scored a touchdown from the 1-yard line. Then they attempted a two-point conversion, but it failed, leaving the score at 12-7. With only three minutes left in the third quarter, Florida's Bentley kicked another field goal to extend the lead 15-7.

At the start of the fourth quarter, Lawrence Phillips, our star running back, scored from the 12-yard line. We also attempted a two-point conversion to tie up the game, but it failed and left FSU still ahead, 15-13. With just one minute, 19 seconds left on the clock, our place kicker, Byron Bennett, kicked a 27-yard field goal. We were now ahead 16-15. The championship was ours for the taking.

Then, the unthinkable happened. With only one minute, 16 seconds left in the game, Florida State's quarterback, Charlie Ward, took control, working his team down the field to the 3-yard line. We were able to hold them there, but with only 21 seconds left in the game, Florida State's Bentley kicked another field goal that once more put the Seminoles in front, 18-16.

Tensions were high and fans were on their feet, screaming, and the roar from the stands was deafening. Confident of their victory, the Florida State team began congratulating each other too early, and was assessed an early celebration penalty of 15 yards on the ensuing kickoff. Nebraska received the ball on the 23-yard line and ran it all the way to the Florida State 43-yard line. The noise was so earsplitting that it is amazing the team could hear Tommie make the calls for the final plays of the game.

Then, Tommie, hit Trumaine Bell, a receiver in mid-field. He made it to the 28-yard line before being tackled, as the clock ran down to nothing but zeros. Again, Florida State thought that the game was won, but the officials put one second back on the clock. The pressure was so intense by now that the screaming fans were ready to burst onto the field. Everyone was out of their seats, straining to see how this classic battle would end as place kicker, Bryon Bennett, made his way onto the field. Bryon lined up to kick what would be the 45 yard winning field goal. All eyes watched as the ball left the ground, careening through the sky towards the goalpost that would confirm our well-deserved championship. But it sailed wide to the left and missed the uprights completely.

Nebraska finished with an 11-1 season. It was tough to lose that game, but I had played in a championship. I knew this was only the beginning for me. I returned to Lincoln ready to skip all of the offseason and begin preparing and practicing for the next championship game. I was determined to play a big part in getting us there.

Traveling to Florida had a special effect on me. It was the first time I had seen the ocean and walked in sand on a beach. I went swimming and just marveled at how big the ocean was. While the team was at the hotel in Miami, I went outside by myself and just stood, watching the waves. As I stood there on the sand and watched the tide move closer and closer towards me, the massiveness of the ocean overwhelmed me, and I felt so small. I thought to myself how amazing it was that a poor boy from Oklahoma actually had the opportunity to drink in the beauty of this moment. Even today, I can still remember the first time I felt the soft sand under my feet and the coolness of an unseen breeze rushing past me as I walked along the beach.

Training camp in the summer of 1994 was phenomenal for me. Everything seemed to be going in the right direction as I began my sophomore year. On Sunday August 28th, we played West Virginia at East Rutherford, New Jersey, and won 31-0. I was making plays all over the field, and even got some interceptions. When we returned to Nebraska the team got a lot of attention and I thought, man, I love this. Everyone loves me. I'm a big man on campus. The world is mine for the taking. Ah, what a life!

Kim found out she was pregnant and we moved in together at her parents' house. I'm not sure how Debbie and Dan took the news-I wasn't there when Kim told them. Later, we learned that Debbie was also pregnant and was due only three months after our baby. At this point in time, I was not even considering marriage. I guess I reasoned that after, I finished school and got a job, we would be married. There were no definite plans, though. I knew I loved Kim, but I was a long way from being ready to make that kind of commitment.

The impending birth did make me more anxious to complete my eligibility and for Kim and I to move on to bigger and better things in our lives. I can remember thinking to myself, I can play my sophomore and junior years, then go on to the NFL. That was my plan, and the first game that year was right on target with my NFL goal. The next game was on Thursday, September 8, 1994, at Texas Tech, played in Lubbock, Texas and televised on ESPN. I was beginning my sophomore year on national television. Wow, I thought!

Tech was supposed to be a tough team, but we were too, so I knew both teams would be playing hard to win. As the game progressed, it appeared that the contest we anticipated was not going to be as hard-fought as we initially thought. We were winning hands-down. In the second half, Tech handed the ball off to run it back to break the line of scrimmage. I ran up to make a tackle, but my foot got caught in the turf wrong and I heard my knee pop…actually, it was a lot less like a pop than it was like a loud crack. I finished the tackle and rolled my opponent off me, but my knee kept popping and crunching and making all sorts of terrible noises, I knew beyond a doubt that something was terribly wrong. I had never felt like that before. I remember lying there, looking up at the sky, thinking, man, this is unbelievable! Football is gone! Then, another thought crept into my mind. If football is gone, what is my life about? If football is what my life is all about, it's gone. I don't have it anymore. Then what's the meaning of my life, if that's not it?

My whole life had been about football. Football was what defined me. I was a football player. That was what gave me satisfaction and fulfillment. I never thought it would be gone so quickly. Then the reality hit me that football, especially a career in football, is very fragile. It's not a guarantee.

It seemed like an eternity, but it was only a couple of moments before the coaches arrived and began checking my knee. They took me to the sidelines and checked it again. I was screaming in pain, but now I think I was screaming more from fear than from the pain. I was scared. Football was my life. What was going happen to me now? To make matters worse, and as if to confirm my worst fears, a coach whispered in my ear, "Son, your football season is over. You're going to have to have surgery on that knee."

I was crushed. I sat there on the bench with a towel over my head, just crying. Despite my attempts to hide my disappointment from the world, the television cameras kept focusing on me on that bench, and the announcers said how important I was for the team. Here I was at the end of my football career and it was all being reported on national television. The only thing missing was the eulogy. I was certain it was all over because, at that time, players didn't come back as easily from ACL surgeries. Not like players today.

On the flight back to Lincoln, I sat in the front of the plane with my leg elevated to help diminish the pain. I didn't want to talk to anyone. While the rest of the team celebrated our 42-16 victory, I could think about nothing but football being over for me. I was so down in the dumps and depressed. Only a few hours before, I had eagerly planned my future. Now I didn't have any idea where my future would take me.

Coach Osborne tried to alleviate my fears and made sure that I was as comfortable as I could be during the plane ride.

"Son, your leg is going to be fine. After the surgery, you'll be back on the field in no time. Now, don't worry, just concentrate on coming back next season."

"I don't know coach," I said as I shook my head. "I've seen too many good players that went down like this and never were able to recuperate."

"I've seen plenty that did come back," Coach said. "It just depends on the stuff you're made of, and I know how tough you are, Mike."

He patted me on my shoulder and somehow I knew he was right. As I reflect on Coach Osborne and my years at Nebraska, I understand why he was such an inspiration to the guys he coached and why they respected him so much.

My surgery was scheduled for two weeks later. During that time, I ambled about on crutches and tried to keep from thinking about the fears that were beginning to consume my every waking moment. I was in pain and fearful that the surgery would not produce the desired results... that I could play football...really competitive football...once again.

Unexpectedly, the day before the operation, Kim asked me to go visit a little boy that her aunt knew. The boy's name was Joshua Molacek. He had been diagnosed with a brain tumor and was not expected to live much longer. Kim said he had asked to meet me, so we went over to his house and talked with him and his family. During our conversation, Joshua told me I was one of his favorite players. Feelings of guilt began to seep into my consciousness. I sat in this boy's home, thinking about how his family must feel. Joshua had a twin sister. How would his family overcome the grief of losing Joshua when, day after day his memory would be aroused by the presence of his surviving sibling? How would his sister deal with the fact that her brother died, yet she survived? A boy that had not even begun to live yet, was about to die, and I was concerned about having knee surgery. The trivial nature of my own self-pity began to change my attitude.

Joshua Molacek's situation inspired and motivated me to realize that I could overcome this injury and get back into football. We connected with each other that night and began a relationship I will never forget.

As Kim and I were about to leave his house, Joshua looked at me and said, "You know, I really appreciate you coming over here. You know what? I'm going to let you borrow my angels when you go into surgery tomorrow. I'll let you borrow them for a little bit so you won't be afraid."

I thought at the time that it was so sweet of him to say that and I said to him, "Thanks, Josh, I appreciate that."

I didn't really think anymore about it when I went into the surgery, but afterwards, I had absolutely no pain. My knee felt great. Then I remembered that Josh had told me he'd loan me his angels, and I knew that something really special had happened during the operation.

Joshua had a profound effect on me, spiritually, and we visited him frequently during the next few months. Then, after a valiant battle, he finally met Jesus and his angels, face-to-face on Christmas Day, 1994. When our son was born the following April, 1995, we named him Michael Joshua as a tribute to the boy who had loaned me his angels so I wouldn't be afraid.

As a result of my time with the Molacek family, I began going to the Fellowship of Christian Athletes meetings (FCA). I went to Bible studies and read the Bible. It was the first book I read completely, cover to cover. Through Joshua and his faith, I began to see the power of God, and to remember how evident it was in my Grandma Nettie's life.

However, my first son, Michael, was born before I had a relationship with Christ as my Savior, and his arrival also played a significant part in my decision to allow Jesus into my life. As I held my newborn son in my arms, I began to really understand how precious life is. I realized during those moments, that the deep love I felt for Michael, could not be compared to the love that Jesus had for me. I was overwhelmed by the sense of love and peace that God had brought into my life through my new family. It was that peace and joy that drew me closer and closer to my destiny. As with everything that God has done in my life, the timing could not have been more perfect.

That year was probably one of the most physically and emotionally painful in my college career. I had been injured in September and was unable to play football for the rest of the season. Then, Joshua died. When Nebraska went to the Orange Bowl for the championship game on January 1, 1995, I was able to travel with the team, but unable to participate. It was a bittersweet time for me.

The Cornhuskers were 12-0 and ranked No.1 in the Associated Press football poll. This time, we played the Miami Hurricanes, ranked No. 3, at the Orange Bowl in Miami, Florida. Tommie Frazier started the game. However, after he threw an interception in the first quarter, Coach Osborne replaced him with backup quarterback, Brook Berringer. Brook had been the starting quarterback during most of the regular season after Tommie suffered a blood clot and was pulled from the roster.

Miami scored the first points on a field goal by Dane Prewitt. Then Trent Jones caught a pass from Canes quarterback, Frank Costa, and scored. That gave Miami a 10-0 lead. During the second quarter, Nebraska finally got on the board when Brook hit Mark Gilman for a 19-yard touchdown pass right before halftime. Miami answered in the third quarter with a 44-yard pass to Jonathan Harris to make the score 17-7. A short time later we struck back when the Hurricanes' quarterback was sacked in the end zone for a safety by linebacker, Dwayne Harris. The third quarter ended with a 17-9 lead by Miami. In a surprising move during the fourth quarter, Coach Osborne decided to return Tommie to the field and a crowd of cheering fans. He quickly passed to Lawrence Phillips, who got the ball to the 15-yard line. Under tremendous pressure,

Tommie threw the ball to Corey Schlesinger, who ran it in for a touchdown. A two-point conversion pass to Eric Alford, made score was now dead even at 17-17.

The Hurricanes were unable to muster any sustained offense, but Tommie continued the comeback effectively, moving the ball into scoring territory. With only five minutes and eight seconds left in the game, we had a third and three mid-field. With no open receiver, Tommie ran for 25 yards to get the first down and more. Then, in the final play of the drive, he found Corey Schlesinger once again at the 14-yard line, and Schlesinger turned it upfield against a worn-out Hurricanes' defense to make the score 24-17. As the clock ticked off the final seconds of the game, our "blackshirt" defense held Miami in check, and the rest is history. The fans were on their feet screaming with excitement…at least the Nebraska faithful were.

In spite of the fact that Tommie only completed three of five passes in the game, he rushed for 25 yards and two of those passes were touchdowns, which led Nebraska to its first national title since 1972. On January 1, 1972 year we won the 1971 Division 1-A championship with a 38-6 win over the University of Alabama and claimed back-to-back National Championship titles. As we did in 1971, we ended the 1993 season, 13-0.

That was also the last year that the Orange Bowl was actually played at the Orange Bowl stadium. In 1996, the championship game was moved to Dolphin Stadium. For me, the moment was bittersweet. Officially, I was a member of a National Championship team. That had always been a part of the dream that had brought me to Nebraska. I was part of the team, yet I wasn't really part of the victory. I was thrilled and disappointed all at the same time. That was the year I had anticipated would be my best. It was the year I had planned to show my talent to the world of collegiate football. Instead, I sat on the sidelines and cheered while other players took my place on the roster. It made me even more determined to resume my rightful place on the team. I would never give up, I told myself. I would succeed, no matter what the odds.

By the summer of 1995, I realized that I wanted a relationship with Jesus Christ. I wanted to be on His team. I needed that relationship. I couldn't live without it. Finally, the question that had lingered for so long in my mind about the meaning of my life was being answered by God. He was telling me that, "It's through my Son and your relationship with Him that you can truly be fulfilled. This is the meaning of your life. It is to know Him and to tell other people about Him."

Man, you couldn't shut me up after that. I was so fired up about Jesus that if you sat down next to me, you were going to find out about Him. I was turning into a one-man evangelist. This was the real journey I'd been looking for all my life, and my bags were packed. I was ready to go!

Kim and I had been living together more than a year and had a son, but I was still not ready for a marriage commitment. I had always told Kim, that we'd get married when I made it to the NFL or got a job after college.

As my walk and relationship with Christ continued to grow, God spoke to my heart and said, "Michael, I just want you to trust me. You just do what you're supposed to do. You already took on the responsibility of marriage when you both had a baby."

Then God reminded me of the story of Joseph and Mary and how Joseph had to trust God. Mary and Joseph weren't married when Mary became pregnant and Joseph must have thought about what everyone would say about him. But God told him not to worry, it was okay. Joseph needed to have faith and to trust in God. That's what God was asking me to do.

So I said, "Okay, God, I'm going to do it!" I have found that when God speaks, I need to listen and obey. It was one of the first things I learned in my walk with Him. He has the map. We just need to follow His directions. Be patient and listen for the next move. He is always faithful to tell you what it is.

I went to Kim and told her that we needed to get married. At that time, she was still not saved and was totally surprised by my change-of-heart.

"What? Are you playing me?" She responded, somewhat dumbfounded by my proposal.

"No, I said. God told me we needed to get married."

"Yeah," she said in a manner that made me think she had been waiting for this day for a long time.

It didn't take long to find the perfect setting for our wedding. It was a beautiful grassy park on the University of Nebraska East Campus. The tree-lined campus which shadowed the quaint little, white, gazebo was perfect for the ceremony.

Two weeks later, on July 29, 1995, Thad Turner, my best man and I, stood waiting on by the gazebo. Thad had married his high school sweetheart, Tonya, as soon as he graduated in 1992, and now had children of his own.

"Are you nervous?" Thad asked. "Man, I can't believe you're about to get married.

There was a time when I thought you would never make a commitment that serious. This is a big step for you."

I chuckled as Thad's reflection took me back to our teens when our focus was on how many girlfriends we could have at one time, without any of them knowing about the other.

"Yeah," I said. "There was a time when I thought the same thing."
I shifted from foot to foot nervously waiting for the ceremony to begin and wondered where Kim and I would be in 10 years, and what our marriage would be like. I knew God had spoken to me about getting married, but I still wasn't quite sure that I knew what He expected from me. After all, it wasn't like I had a role model that I could look at and say "I want my marriage to be just like my dad's and mom's."

"Just trust Me," God had said. "I'll make sure you learn how to be a good husband and father." Without His assurance I would have never had the courage to take that leap of faith.

It was a hot day, and I had opted for the men to just wear vests instead jackets. Our families and many of our friends were there to help us celebrate this occasion. Almost overnight, it had become one of the most spiritual events of my entire life.

Then, the music began to play and Stephanie Molacek, Joshua's twin sister, walked slowly down the isle. Kim had asked her to be the flower girl. Following slowly behind Stephanie, Stephanie Knittle, a life-long friend, attended Kim as her maid-of-honor. Finally, "Mendelssohn's Wedding March" began to play. As

Kim appeared, my world became even brighter. I looked down the isle and saw her coming towards me in the most beautiful white dress I had ever seen in my life. She actually glowed, and I thought God had touched her with His glory. Her long, blond, curly hair lying softly on her shoulders, made her look just like an angel floating carelessly towards me. She was so beautiful that she took my breath away.

Reverend Scott Pixler, the music minister at Capital City Christian Church, performed the ceremony. Afterwards, everyone was invited to the Roses' home for a small reception. That evening, we left three-month old Michael with his grandparents, and Kim and I took a short honeymoon that consisted of one night in a nice hotel, somewhere in Lincoln.

I can truly say that God has blessed our marriage. Kim was and continues to be my companion, my best friend, my love and my balance. She is truly one of the best gifts God has ever given to me.

I had begun a new journey in my life, and I was refreshed. Now, I looked forward with anticipation for the new football season to begin.

Chapter 5

CAPTURING THE NFL'S ATTENTION

It isn't about how many times you're knocked down.
It's about how many times you get up and try again.

The 1995 season opened with Nebraska at the Boone Pickens Stadium in Stillwater, Oklahoma, where we trounced Oklahoma State 64-21. My surgery had gone well, with little or no pain. I had a wife who supported me fully in my goals to reach the NFL, and a new son. What could be better?

By the third game against Arizona State, though, my knee started hurting. I couldn't seem to run the way I had before because of the pain, and I had no strength in my leg. That game was bad for me because I couldn't produce for the team the way I had previously.

I found myself afraid and depressed again. I kept thinking, I was not coming back from this injury the way I thought I would. To make matters worse, on the Sunday after the game, Kim came to me with the newspaper in her hand. I could tell she was angry by the expression on her face.

"Have you read the paper?" she asked.

"No," I said, taking it from her hand.

"The coach is saying you're washed up. You can't play anymore," Kim said. I read the article about the game, especially where defensive coach, Charlie McBride, had commented on my performance from the night before. "When Mike Minter is healthy, he is the best, McBride said, "but, he just can't do it anymore. He's washed up," the article continued.

It was definitely another turning point because that comment fired me up and made me mad. I was even more determined to come back to the performance levels I had displayed before the injury. The next day at practice I hit as hard as I could and ran as fast as possible. I wanted show the coaches that I could still play as well as I had before blowing my knee out. McBride's comment only motivated me to overcome the pain and prove him wrong. The thing about negative comments is that people have a very clear choice about how to react to them. For some, the negativity deflates their egos. They buy into what they have been told and move on to a new endeavor. Unfortunately, these kinds of people often look back on their lives and wonder what might have been. I saw negative comments as a challenge to prove the critics wrong.

What was my strategy? At first I just blocked the pain out. Then, later, either it subsided or I just got used to it. I'm not sure what happened.

As the 1995 season drew to a close, we were rated No. 1 by the Associated Press (AP). We were invited to the Fiesta Bowl, to be held January 2, 1996 at the Sun Devil Stadium in Tempe, Arizona. In this national championship game, we were pitted against University of Florida (UF) which was ranked No. 2 in the AP.

This matchup came about through the newly formed Bowl Alliance, which had the national championship game rotate between the Orange, Sugar, and Fiesta Bowls. This year the championship game belonged to the Fiesta Bowl. In the old system, Nebraska would have been tied to the Orange Bowl and Florida to the Sugar Bowl.

The Florida Gators, under head coach, Steve Spurrier, had developed the nickname "fun n gun," because their success was predicated on how well they threw the ball and their team speed. It was how they had achieved so much of there success during the season. Consistent with their reputation, they threw the ball a lot in that game, too.

One of the things I remember the most was their first drive. They went all the way down the field, but our defense stiffened and we held them to three points. I remember coming off the field and saying to one of the guys on the sideline, "That's the best they got? They went all the way down the field and all they got was three points? They're in trouble tonight."

From that point on, we totally dominated the game. Our defense was blitzing so much that the Gator's offense had to be wondering whether they should head for the end zone or the showers.

We knew the game was over, even before halftime. It was such a blow-out. I remember one play in particular. We had a coverage call, but our linebackers were blitzing and that wasn't the plan. I was yelling and trying to get our defenders to realize that someone had screwed up the play call. I remember thinking that this could be a bad play. I knew we would need to get to the quarterback or they would have somebody wide open. That could end with the real possibility of them scoring a momentum-turning touchdown. On that particular play, Florida had two people going out for a pass, and our linebackers were preparing to blitz. That left me with two people to cover. Luckily, one of our linebackers, Jamel Williams, got the sack. In fact, he crashed through the offensive line and brought the quarterback down so quickly that he had no chance to set up and deliver a pass. He never had a chance to look for the two people who were open.

Throughout that game, I had really bad cramps. Finally, Coach took me out for a couple of plays, and Eric Stokes took my place. He ended up with a big interception. I was happy he was able to stop the play, but I was mad at myself because that could have been me catching that pass. Another highlight of that game was when Tommie Frazer, rushed 75 yards for a touchdown.

The way things were going, we knew that game was won long before it was over, so we were all on the sidelines celebrating. Even though I didn't make any big plays in that game, it was the first championship game that I had the opportunity to participate in, and I was excited about that.

The final score was 62-24 and we ended the year 12-0. I was credited with 53 tackles, two interceptions and six deflected passes, and I also earned All-Big Eight second-team recognition. What a difference a year can make in the life of a football player. Just one year ago I had been wondering if I would even play football again. Now, here I was sitting on top of the collegiate football world.

Nebraska's opening game in 1996 was with Michigan State we got off to a good start with a 55-14 victory. That game was especially memorable for me. Not only did I play against my future friend and Panther teammate, Muhsin Muhammad, it was also the game in which I scored my first touchdown. I will always remember that play. From the time that the quarterback let the ball go, I knew I had him. I caught the ball and raced 70 yards down the sidelines. As I ran, I thought to myself, this is a great way to open the '96 season. Many times people asked me when I really thought that I had a shot at the NFL. It was during that game. When I was running down that field, in my mind I was running toward a career in the NFL. From that point on, everything I did on the field was to capture their attention.

The next week, however, we lost to Arizona State in Phoenix, 19-0. It was our only loss during regular season football. During the rest of the schedule, we beat all our opponents and made it look easy. Teams like Colorado State went down 65-9; Kansas State, 39-3; and a shut-out to Baylor 49-0. We destroyed Oklahoma, our traditional rival, 73-21. The Nebraska Cornhuskers were invulnerable...or so we thought.

Nineteen ninety-six was a monumental year in college football. It was the first year of The Big 12 Championship game. The Big 12 Conference had evolved with the merging of the original Big Eight Conference schools and four Texas schools that had been members of the disbanded Southwest Conference. All 12 schools are located in the central United States.

In this championship game the North Division champion was to be pitted against the South Division champion. On November 29, 1996, we played Colorado in the Big 12 North Division Championship game. It was an important game for us because, essentially, it was the first of three potential championship games that year, and we intended to win them all.

It also marked a change in position for me. After playing almost exclusively in the defensive backfield for my entire collegiate career, I found myself having to make an adjustment to linebacker in a championship game. Sometime during that week, a linebacker for Nebraska had gotten into trouble and was kicked off the team. I was not used to playing that close to the line of scrimmage, so I had a lot to learn quickly. Changing positions on defense may not seem very complicated, but unlike backyard football where a player simply chooses which player he is responsible for covering, the plays involved in Division-I football are much more complex. At this level, each defender has a number of responsibilities and, as the play develops, those responsibilities may change rapidly. This requires not only a different mindset, but different positioning of the body as well, in order to follow through and execute a scheme designed to thwart the opposing offense. It wasn't that I didn't have confidence in my abilities, I was just nervous that I might get caught out of position in a play that might cost us the game. Fortunately, we pulled it off and came away with a 17-12 win, but the weather was cold and rainy. As a result, many of the guys on the team got sick and weren't able to practice the next week for the upcoming game against the Texas Longhorns.

Our game plan was essentially to continue doing what we had done in the Colorado game, and previously during our phenomenal season. In our minds that would be sufficient to beat a team that in our estimation, wasn't that good. We went into that game with a 10-1 record, and Texas was 7-4. We were ranked No. 3 at that time in the AP poll, and they were No. 20. It was a no-contest game in our minds.

December 7, 1996 turned out to be our own "day that would live in infamy." We came to the Trans World America Stadium as the heavy favorite to win. Coach Osborne put me in as a linebacker again. We were getting beaten deep, but it went back and forth, back and forth. Texas couldn't stop us offensively and we couldn't stop them. We were able to stop their star running back, Ricky Williams, but Priest Holmes came out of nowhere and had a big game against us.

The score was 30-27, Texas, in the fourth quarter. With only two minutes and forty seconds to play in the game, we were able to stop them on a critical third down. The Longhorns were on their own 28-yard line with a fourth down and inches. Nebraska called its last timeout for this play and Texas decided to go for it. They knew that if they punted the ball for a field goal, we were going to get the ball back and score because they couldn't stop our offense anymore than we had been able to stop theirs.

Texas quarterback, James Brown, was getting his final instructions from their coach, John Mackovic. Finally, the whistle blew and they came into a formation where they had two tight ends in formation. Our whole defense was packed in the middle of the field. Everyone thought they were going to run a quarterback sneak, or at least we thought they were going to run the ball up the middle. They had a full backfield power set with three people in the backfield. In this game we had a freshman corner, Ralph Brown, who had played phenomenally during the season and was having a pretty good game that night as well. He was lined up in the "A" gap between the center and the guards. He was supposed to cover the tight end man-to-man, but, at that moment, Ralph wasn't concentrating on the tight end. He was more worried about that quarterback sneak, but it was the sneak that never materialized.

The Longhorns' quarterback got the ball and rolled out to the left. At the same time, all the running backs came to the line of scrimmage. Meanwhile, I rolled with the quarterback, knowing if we could stop them we would get the ball back and score. I came toward Brown as he moved his arm back to pass. I jumped a little bit, but didn't want to commit because I thought he was trying to fake me. He threw the ball over my head and I was wondering who he was throwing it to. Then I looked behind me and there was their tight end, Derek Lewis, who was wide open to receive it. Jamel Williams, one of our linebackers, caught him at the 11-yard line and tried to strip the ball from him, but he couldn't. The Texans had gained 61 yards on that single play. It was a great call and well executed, and I really had to respect them for it, but I didn't have to like it. At that moment I wished we hadn't even allowed them into our conference. On the next play, Priest Holmes took the ball into the end zone, giving Texas a 37-27 lead to put a cap on the game.

The loss was significant. It was the first championship game in three years that we had not come out the victor. I was so mad. We lost that game because our defense had failed at a critical point in the game. That was a very low point in my life. I was so depressed that I didn't want to go outside, or eat, shave, or do anything. I was upset because it was my senior year and a year when we had a chance to win three championships in a row. We gave up one of those championships to a team that really wasn't that good. In fact, Texas ended their season, 8-5 and ranked No. 23 in the AP poll.

It took me from early December until we played Virginia Tech in the Orange Bowl to get over that game. It was a game I thought that could have literally changed my life and the lives of other players. That's how much I wanted to win that game. This was an experience that I was destined to relive over and over, during my years with the NFL.

Even now, when Coach Osborne and I get together, he still says to me, "Mike, I'm sorry for making that move. I should have put you back at safety and we would have beaten Texas if I had done that." We all relive that game, not just me. Today, you could probably ask anyone that was on that Nebraska team about that game and they'd break down and start crying. It was that tough.

During that time, I began paying attention to all the sports publications that carried predictions about the upcoming NFL draft season. I wanted to read everything I could find regarding who they thought were the best safeties. I watched television sports shows to see what they were saying about me. Just like every other guy who dreamed of the NFL, I wanted that stamp of approval...the validation indicating that others in the sports information circle recognized my potential as a professional football player. It was important to me to know if the sports commentators thought I could make it in the NFL. They ranked me the fifth safety likely to be drafted, so I began to believe that I had a chance to make it. Then the Mel Kiper Jr. report listed me as a potentially high draft pick, so I became more and more confident that I would be able to play pro football. I thought about these predictions and they continued to help me focus on playing well.

The 1997 FedEx Orange Bowl Game was played on December 31, 1996 at Pro Player Stadium in Miami Gardens, Florida. In the first quarter Virginia Tech's quarterback, Jim Druckenmiller, threw a touchdown pass to give Virginia a 7-0 lead. Then, in the second quarter Nebraska scored with a field goal by Kris Brown and a touchdown by Scott Frost, giving us a 10-7 lead. Just before halftime, Nebraska's Jason Peter recovered a fumble and returned it for a touchdown. We were now ahead 17-7. Virginia, however, took possession of the ball and Druckenmiller threw a touchdown pass to Shaw Scales with only 19 seconds left in the half. Nebraska was still ahead at the half, although our lead had been cut to 17-14.

Early in the third quarter, Nebraska scored another touchdown, but Virginia answered with a 33-yard touchdown pass to Cornelius White. The score was now 24-21. That was the last we would hear from the Hokies' offense, however. We scored another touchdown to end the third quarter and another touchdown after that one, plus a field goal in the fourth quarter. We came out the winner in that hard-fought championship. The final score was 41-21, and it was the last official game of my college career so I was happy that we had won. We ended the season 11-2 that year. In that game alone I made about 18 tackles because I was still so mad about the Longhorns game. Not bad for a safety converted to linebacker trying to capture the attention of an NFL team! That, at least, took some of the sting out of losing that Big 12 Conference game.

During my last year of eligibility, I made 51 tackles, produced five interceptions, deflected six passes and was credited with five quarterback rushes. I even ran one pass back for a touchdown. At the end of my collegiate career, I had earned a place in Big 12 first-team honors.

Since I had begun playing for Nebraska in my true freshman year, 1993, we had only lost three games. I had become accustomed to playing on a winning team, so, I never considered that my professional career would be any different. I could not have foreseen that in one year my career would take such an abrupt turn.

College eligibility had ended with the regular season in November. Agents who had been patiently waiting on the sidelines began to approach me. Many agents, however, began scouting the most likely draftees covertly in the fall of their last year of eligibility. They can't legally talk with the draft prospect, but they get around that by talking with the family or relatives who act as middlemen until they can talk freely with the athlete.

Between November 1996 and January 1997, I interviewed with about three agents. The reality is that there isn't enough time to choose an agent that best fits your needs. The Senior Bowl was coming up January 1997, and the NFL

Scouting Combine right afterwards. I needed an agent to help me prepare.

The antiquated rules had been designed with the idea that college football players didn't have to worry about signing with an agent until the NFL draft. But, today, NFL teams are taking a much more active role in determining who they might target in April. In fact, the NFL Combine has become an event unto itself.

At this point, your agent's role is to provide you with information. They are the ones who give you an itinerary and literally tell you where you need to be and when you need to be there. Once you are at the post-season games, your agent is responsible for talking with the teams and giving you feedback as to which teams are interested in drafting you. Therefore from January to the NFL draft in April, he is finding out what the individual NFL teams think about you. The more information you know about what is going on behind the scenes, the less anxious you feel and the better you are able to determine where you will fall in the draft. It is critical to choose an agent that can give you the best advice…advice that you need sooner, not later.

It is a mind-boggling experience, so I decided to call my high school teammate, Daryl Gardener, who had chosen Baylor over Nebraska, to help me with that decision. He'd begun his eligibility immediately during his freshman year. Consequently, he had graduated a year before I did and was picked by the Miami Dolphins in Round One of the 1996 draft. I was confident that Daryl knew the ropes and I leaned heavily on his advice for an agent. That's why I chose Neil Swartz.

Swartz was my agent during my first four-year contract. He represented a lot of big name sports stars, such as Terrell Davis, a running back for the Denver Broncos. Some agents want to help you with everything. They negotiate your signing bonus and your contract. They also want to be your financial advisor, but I didn't want that. I wanted to have a separate financial advisor, apart from my sports agent, so I again went to Daryl for advice about a financial advisor and chose Ken Ready of Prudential, who also handled Daryl's investments.

For new draft prospects, the period of time between the end of your college eligibility and the draft the following spring can be very precarious. Many prospects, like me, went to college on a scholarship. In most cases they don't have two nickels to rub together. Kim worked at a daycare during this period of time. It was something she enjoyed very much and it brought in a much needed income into our family.

After living paycheck-to-paycheck for so long we had now reached a point where we could look forward to a very lucrative job in the near future-possibly. However, it is sometimes very hard to wait to receive the benefits you have worked so long to achieve. And, it is also difficult to understand how to manage the amount of money that as a young athlete, you are on the brink of earning. An agent steps in at this point to help a potential draftee transition to this new environment.

One of the selling points that an agent makes to a new prospect is that he is able to get loans that you can borrow against. These loans anticipate a signing bonus that you receive when you're finally drafted. The loan is repaid from the bonus, after you receive your first check. That's where some draftees can get into trouble. No one can ever be sure exactly where they will be picked in the draft until it actually happens. Therefore, it's impossible to be sure of what money you're going to receive. Initially, in order to anticipate the percentage of the signing bonus you might get, the agent will begin by trying to determine where you will fall in the draft. At that point he looks at the bonus for someone in your position that got drafted last year.

As for Kim and I, we decided that we needed a car and we chose to move out of her parents' house into a rented studio apartment in November, 1996. That was the extent of our purchases based on a future signing bonus. By then, Michael was a toddler and Kim was pregnant with our second child, Isaiah. Now the wait began for our hopes and dreams to materialize

Some draftees will go out and spend a lot of money they don't have yet. Then, in the draft, they don't receive what they had hoped. In some cases they are drafted beyond the third round, or even as a free agent and receive little or no bonus at all. It's a risk to the agents, too. Once the draft actually begins, the bonuses for the first players chosen set the benchmark for everyone else.

Orlando Pace, a left tackle from Ohio State, was the first pick in the 1997 draft. He was the first offensive lineman in 30 years to be taken as a first pick. Pace was drafted by the St. Louis Rams. Originally, he was offered a six-year contract for $24.7 million, with $9.5 million guaranteed. However, after sitting out most of the 1997 training camp, he finally settled for a $25.6-million deal that would allow him to opt out after three years.

By the time Rae Carruth, a wide receiver from Colorado, was drafted as the 27th pick by Carolina in the first round, the signing bonus had dwindled to $3.7 million. The higher up in the draft you are selected-the better your opportunity for a very substantial bonus.

The Senior Bowl was held on January 26, 1997, at the Ladd Peebles Stadium in Mobile, Alabama. The bowl is actually a charitable event sponsored by a nonprofit organization called the Mobile Arts & Sports Association.

It was an exciting experience for me because the two teams, named the North and the South, are coached by NFL team coaches. That year the coaches were Norv Turner, from the Washington Redskins, coaching the North, and Marty Schottenheimer, from the Kansas City Chiefs, coaching the South team. I played on the North team. The biggest thing I remember was that I finally had a chance to play with the guys that were considered the best of the best in college football that year. I was really excited about matching up with those guys.

Also, the NFL personnel and my agent were not sure whether I should play corner or safety. I had the speed for corner and I wasn't the typical safety size and build, but I was able to hit hard. So throughout the practice I played both corner and safety.

The game is preceded by a week of practice that is attended by NFL personnel- teams, coaches, scouts and general managers who are there to see the potential prospects for the upcoming NFL draft in the spring. However, many of them leave before the actual All- Star game. They aren't really interested in the game; they mainly want to watch the one-on-one drills during practice.

At first, I didn't like the fact that I had to play corner. I wanted to play safety. I was the most comfortable in that position. I knew that corners made a lot of money. So I thought, if I have to play corner, I will. It was a good opportunity for me to prove that I could play either position.

That year the game had a sellout crowd of 40,646 people. The South scored first with a touchdown run by Jay Graham, but the North answered with three touchdown passes by Pat Barnes, who was named the MVP player that year. At halftime the lead for the North was 21-7. Then in the second half, George Jones, playing for the North, scored two touchdowns. The South's quarterback Jake Plummer finally retaliated with a pass to David LaFleur who scored to make the final score 35-14. Once again, I was on a winning team and I felt my future was becoming more and more secure.

After the Senior Bowl, I was invited to attend the NFL Scouting Combine held at the Hoosier Dome in Indianapolis, Indiana. Only 300 players are chosen to go to Indianapolis and almost all of those will be drafted. It is mind-boggling that out of the thousands of athletes who are eligible for the draft from various colleges and universities, the field of those chosen for the NFL each year is reduced to less than 300 players. I was happy to be chosen for the Combine because it gave me a chance to see my competition. It was at this point that I started feeling really good about my chances.

The Combine allows professional sports personnel to look at individual players, not just for their athletic abilities, but to determine their cognitive abilities as well. It gives them a chance to get to know the prospects better to determine how they might fit with a particular team. There is even a psychological analysis done to determine what prospects are more likely to become a high-maintenance risk to a team. How much weight these tests are given in a player's selection is determined by individual teams.

For example, Pete Williams, in his book, "The Draft," relates that the NFL goes as far back as the eighth grade looking for information that gives them insight into the character of a player. He goes on to relate that when Tony Dungy was coach of the Tampa Bay in 1995, he looked for "solid citizen players who managed to perform beyond their physical capabilities'." Williams said that "Dungy avoided players that had run-ins with the law." Dungy was fired by Tampa Bay in 2001 and replaced by John Gruden, who took the opposite approach and chose players whose on-field performance was outstanding, regardless of any character flaws. According to Williams, "Gruden could overlook off-the-field transgressions, even lobbying during the 2003 season for the Bucs to sign Darrell Russell, whose rap sheet included a suspension for violating the league's substance abuse policy and rape charges that were dismissed."

Also, in an article written by Mike Freeman for *The New York Times*, in April, 1997, the New York Giants looked closely at the psychological tests of Ike Hilliard, Yatil Green and Rae Carruth. Although Hilliard might not have had Carruth's speed or Green's size, they chose him over the others. Why? Because, Freeman states, "Green, who was picked 15th by the Miami Dolphins, had what one general manager called 'off-the-field issues' and Carruth may have had some character issues as well. In fact, several people who were close to the situation said both players did not fair well on the Giants' psychological test." As a result, a shocked Hilliard, who was clearly not listed as a top 10 pick, was the first wide receiver taken in the 1997 draft, by the Giants.

The "Pro Days" arrived in March. During this time NFL teams send staff to the various schools to talk with the players. The Carolina Panthers brought their whole staff to Lincoln, but never talked with me. I visited the New York Jets, Washington Redskins and Chicago Bears on recruiting trips so I thought those teams were serious about me. At one point I even thought I might go to Tampa Bay or the New England Patriots.

April of 1997 was a very eventful time in my life. Isaiah, our second son, was born just two weeks before the NFL draft. By draft day I was so nervous, I was ready to go with whichever team chose me, not that I really had a choice. The 1997 draft had certainly evolved from its initial beginnings in 1936. That year, the number one pick was Jay Berwanger, who played halfback for the University of Chicago. He was also winner of the inaugural Heisman Trophy. In spite of all the efforts to recruit him by the Philadelphia Eagles and the Chicago Bears, Berwanger refused to sign with any NFL team. Instead, he opted for a sports writing career because he could make more money. In fact, out of the original 81 draft picks that year, only 28 actually chose to play professional football, and most of those players left their professional football careers behind by 1940. Today, draft candidates wait anxiously by their phones, each man hoping against hope that his phone will ring with an invitation to join the NFL.

I was no different, as I sat almost motionless and speechless glued to the television on the first day of the draft in April, 1997. All my family was there as I waited. The announcer began with the No. 1 draft pick that year, Orlando Pace. The draft picks were being announced every 15 minutes. Time seemed to stand still for me as the names were announced one by one. I had been waiting to hear the phone ring for over two and a half hours. No safeties had been taken in the first round. That's okay, I thought. I didn't expect to go until the second round anyway. I was also very aware that only a few of the 30 NFL teams that year needed a safety. However, after talking with Swartz, he thought I would be drafted somewhere in the early part of the second round.

Now the second round was beginning. This was my moment I thought. I felt just like I did the night I came home and saw that Tom Osborne was at my house-except that this time there was so much more on the line for me. Now I had a wife and two children to support. My whole life had been spent preparing for this moment. What would I do if the plans I had did not materialize the way I had envisioned they would? I sat anxiously in an old recliner, the telephone only inches from my hand, waiting for the one call that I knew was about to change my life and assure mine and my family's future.

The first pick in the second round went to the New York Jets, who took Rick Terry, a defensive tackle from North Carolina. Then New Orleans chose Rob Kelly, a free safety from Ohio State. Chicago needed a safety, too, but their first pick was John Alred, a tight end from Southern California.

It was getting a little nerve-racking by now. Everyone was trying so hard to stay quiet, but the tension was mounting and the butterflies in my stomach had become wild horses that could not be contained.

Kim and I had already alerted family and friends not to telephone us to find out what was happening. We didn't want anyone tying up the telephone line. I had thought I would get the call early in the second round. The round was well underway and only one safety had been chosen. It appeared that this draft was weighted toward offensive players. I played defense. Three hours had passed as I listened intently for the next name to be called. The 50th draft pick was being announced. He was Mike Logan, a safety from West Virginia, who went to the Jacksonville Jaguars. Things were getting tense for me now. Two safeties had been taken, and I wasn't either of them. I had been so sure that I would be drafted by now. There were only 10 more picks left in the second round and with each pick the signing bonuses and contracts dwindled.

As every name that was not mine was called, I saw my hopes and dreams for my future in professional football slowly being eroded. Would I be one of the hopeful many, whose dreams of playing professional football dwindled and died that day? The pick was at number 55 overall, and the announcer was saying that Marc Edwards, a fullback from Notre Dame had just been chosen by the San Francisco 49ers. I put my head in my hands and prayed, "Please, Father, let me be able to accept your will, not my own."

Then suddenly the phone rang and the voice on the other end said, "Mike? This is Bill Pollian with the Carolina Panthers. Congratulations, son! We're going to pick you as the next pick in the NFL draft. You're going to be a Carolina Panther. How do you feel about being a Carolina Panther?"

My throat was dry and I could hardly make the words form in my mouth. "Yes, yes," was all I could say.

I was so excited. I felt the whole world had just been lifted off my shoulders. Everything I had ever dreamed about and worked for my whole life came true with that one telephone call. I didn't even know where the Panthers played, but I was happy just to be going there. Nevertheless, I was totally surprised because Carolina had never talked to me. Later I learned that Kevin Steele, a linebacker coach for Carolina had also been the linebacker coach for Nebraska during my first few years there, so I figured that had to be the connection. To this day, I believe he was the influence in my being chosen by Carolina.

I spoke with almost everyone connected with the Panthers, from the general manager and president, Bill Pollian, to Coach Dom Capers. They all welcomed me to the team. I was so relieved and happy! I thought, man, they just won the National Football Conference West (NFC West) and they had been only one game away from the Super Bowl. I had been on championship teams all my life so it just made sense to me that I would be on a winning team in the pros, too. I thought to myself, I'm going to the right team. Man, I'm exited! Kim and I immediately researched the location where we would be living. We knew it was in Carolina, but which one, we weren't sure.

Even though Carolina was still a young team, and 1997 was only their third season in the NFL, they had taken professional football by storm. The Panthers won the NFC West, and beat the Dallas Cowboys 26-17 in the 1996 divisional playoffs. However, they lost to the Green Bay Packers 30-13 in the NFC Championship game. This was an unprecedented success for an expansion team. Green Bay went on to win the Super Bowl that year, and the Panthers ended their 1996 season 13-5. Yes, I was more than ready to become part of this team! The draft was behind me now and the relief I felt was immense. All the years of focus and preparation to achieve the goal of playing in professional sports had culminated in that one phone call congratulating me on becoming a Carolina Panther.

Now Neil Swartz would begin a new phase of his job as my agent, that of negotiating my contract and signing bonus. There is little time and so much that goes on behind the scenes at this point between the agents, players and individual teams. Finally the negotiations were complete and I settled for a $1.6 million contract over four years, with a $700,000 signing bonus. The amount of the signing bonus is deducted from the amount of the overall contract, so my yearly salary equated to an additional $225,000 per year. It seemed like an amazing amount of money to two people who just a few months before had a zero bank account.

At this point in an athlete's life, you would think that all their stress about money is over, but it has just begun. From the point that an athlete deposits the signing bonus into his bank account, he acquires more relatives and friends then he had ever known in his life. It is impossible to express the frustration that occurs when all those people began asking for money. Not only is it impossible to give to everyone the amounts he or she is requesting, it's also not practical.

Over the years I have tried to help people, but what I have found is that when you help many of the people that come to you with a hard luck story, those same people will be back the next year, with the same or similar problem. What I had to learn to do, and I encourage new athletes to do the same, is to be discriminating as to that person's actual need. If you help them, and they return again, help them determine a solution to their problem, but don't just keep throwing money into a black hole.

It isn't that most athletes don't want to help relatives and friends; it's that they can't keep giving a handout to the same people over and over. Not only would they deplete their resources, they would be doing a disservice to those people. It's a frustrating situation to have thrust on you and I can tell you from personal experience that the hardest thing in the world to do is to say no to someone close to you. Today, the NFL has classes for the rookies that instruct new recruits how to do just that.

After I signed my first NFL contract, I was finally able to accomplish a lifelong dream that I had, which was to repay my mama for all the hard work and support she had given me all of my life. I knew that her encouragement had been a very vital part of the goals I was able to achieve. I asked Mama what she wanted and she said she wanted a car. So I flew to Oklahoma and took her to the car lot and said, "Pick out your car." She picked out a Nissan and I paid cash for it. She cried and hugged me, saying that she just couldn't believe it. I had always told her that, when I made it, I would always take care of her. That time had finally come. It was the first time that I was really able to do that. I saw the joy and peace in her eyes and those eyes said to me that I had accomplished everything that she had told me I could do ever since I was born. She had always said to me that I would be a success.

I believe that parents often set the kind of path their children are going to take by their own words. Words are such a powerful force and they can build up and encourage, or they can destroy in an instant all the potential that a child may have to become a very successful individual. That day I saw how excited Mama was for me that I had accomplished what I had set out to do. For me, this was a dream come true. It was really bigger than making it to Nebraska or even the NFL. A large part of my dream was the ability to take care of my mama. I wanted to buy her something and I didn't want her to ever have to work again. All those emotions at that moment were because I was able to see a dream come true just the way I had envisioned it.

Yes, I'm a dreamer. I admit it. I sit around and dream about how things are going to be in my life and what I'm going to be doing. Sometimes I live five, 10 or even 15 years into the future. I never really live in the moment. That moment at the car lot with Mama, took me back in time and I thought to myself how, as an eight-year-old child, I had been determined that, one day, I would be able to show my mama the love and appreciation I had for her.

Even in later years, any time that I was afraid I could always call Mama and she would tell me, "Mike, nothing is going to stop you from doing what you are supposed to do. It's going to happen just like it's supposed to." She was always there to encourage me.

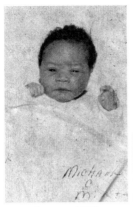

January 1974
Mike at one week

Mama, Chewy, Mike - 1977

Kindergarten 1979

2nd Grade - 1981

7th Grade - 1986

9th Grade Basketball

Senior Picture - 1992

First Car - 1979 Dodge Aspen

High School Heisman
Senior Year - 1992

L-R: Mama's brothers and sisters: Cleve, Loretta,
Mama, Joyce, Leonard, Sandra

High School Graduation - 1992

Mike and "Rerun" - 1993

Miami Florida Orange
Bowl - 1993

Mike holding Michael
Joshua - April 1995

Wedding Bells
July 29, 1995

Championship game
at Nebraska - 1996

Signing autographs at the University
of Nebraska - 1996

Mike posing with Heisman
Trophy at the Orange Bowl

L - R: Isaiah, Mike and Michael
relaxing at home

Mike and Isaiah waiting for surgery - 2002

McKenna (L) and Brianna (R) with dad,
Mike at their pre-school graduation

Meet the Minters: Brianna, Mike,
Kim, Michael, Isaiah, McKenna

Mama, Chewy, Mike and
Roselind - 2005

Chapter 6

THE DOM CAPERS YEARS 1997-1998

Jobs in the NFL are not won or lost, they're given and taken.

I arrived in North Carolina for mini-camp a week after the draft and was paired with Damon Benning to room together. He had been a running back for Nebraska and was picked by the Panthers as a rookie free agent. Damon was eventually cut that year; however, his professional football career took him into the area of indoor football where he was the most prominent player on the IFL Lincoln Lightning team. After about four years the league folded and Damon left professional sports. Today, we still keep in contact and he runs a nonprofit organization in St. Louis, Missouri.

My first exposure to Charlotte was on a bus that carried the new draftees to Ericsson Stadium for our initial training. (The name was changed to Bank of America Stadium in 2005). However, the thing that impressed me most, wasn't the skyline of the city, or the stadium, it was that the whole area was so green. I could not believe how many trees covered the entire region. That night, when I telephoned Kim, she wanted to know how training camp was going but I could not stop talking about those beautiful trees. All my life I had lived in either Oklahoma or Nebraska, and I was used to a flat, treeless environment. To see a green, rolling landscape, with all those trees just confirmed to me that this was where I belonged.

When I arrived at mini-camp in May, 1997, I was convinced we would be going to the Super Bowl, so my whole focus was to be a starter on the team that year. I intended to do whatever I needed to do in order to show the coaches I was ready to play on the first team.

On the first day of training, the coaching staff gave us a playbook about the size of a New York City telephone directory. The information covered a variety of topics including the team philosophy and a review of the Panther defense. Then, we broke into groups where we talked specifically about defensive backs and those positions on the team. In these small groups, we were introduced to basic defenses such as the cover three scheme, the cover two scheme, and the man-to-man scheme. First came classroom instruction, then, we went to practice it. After a short lunch break, we returned to the practice field. Then we went back to the classroom, where the staff gave us some defensive schemes that we were expected to learn by the next day. Each night, when we returned to our hotel rooms, we studied those schemes. For four days the schedule never changed meet and practice, meet and practice.

The routine didn't bother me, but I was anxious to begin the main training camp, which was held in July. I remember looking at the team on the practice field one day and thinking, these guys aren't very good. I thought they were one game away from the Super Bowl. I realized later that none of the veteran players were there, only the rookies. Dom Capers, who had been the head coach since the team started in the league, did not require veteran players to come to mini-camp. It was just for the new players.

Once the veterans arrived during the later camps, I saw a big difference. There is little free time when you are at camp, so I took every spare moment to look for housing. I wanted to move my family to Charlotte as soon as possible.

I returned to Nebraska and prepared to come back to North Carolina for the next camp, which would be held a month later, in June. Almost all the players were there at the June camp, and that is where I was first introduced to Eric Davis.

One particular day we were all on the practice field doing stretches and Eric Davis called out to me, "Hey Nebraska. Nebraska! What are you doing?"

I remember laughing and wondering, who is this guy? He's wrestling with me.

Then Davis said, "Nebraska, this is real football now."

"I'm not worried, because I can handle it," I replied right back at him, trying not to appear intimidated by his harassment. From that day on, Davis teased me all the time. Actually, I believe he liked me from Day One because he saw something in me that revealed a good football player.

Eric Davis became my mentor. He was like Will Shields had been to me in college. He showed me the ropes in the NFL and helped me to understand what the game was really all about. The first thing that caught my attention was how much shorter NFL practice is compared to college football. I guess it's because you don't have as many people.

At the June camp, players live at home and drive to practice each day, which is held at the stadium in Charlotte. But, in the main training camp, held in July, players stay together at camp, which is located at Wofford College in Spartanburg, South Carolina. In June, having no local home, I continued to lodge in a hotel that the Panthers arranged for new players.

I wanted to get Kim and the children settled in Charlotte before that camp, but I knew my time would be very limited, so I spent every minute during my free time looking at housing. Damon Benning actually showed me around Charlotte and helped me look for a house. I remember it being the first time I had ever really seen large, two-story houses. When we rode around, I asked the cost of the different houses we saw. To me, a big house was 2,800 to 3,000 square feet. Until now, I had no exposure to houses that size in either Oklahoma, or Nebraska. So, I was in awe at how big some of those houses were that we looked at in Charlotte. Upon learning they were around $200,000, I found myself saying, "is that all those houses costs? Man, we're going to have us a nice house!"

Granted, many of the new Carolina players were choosing housing in the higher-priced neighborhoods in town. But, I preferred the housing that was available in the University area of Charlotte. It was more modest but I liked the neighborhoods in that area. A house 2,800 square feet might have cost $200,000 in that area. The same size house in the south end of town went for $500,000, mainly because of location. I finally settled on a house located in a subdivision called Prosperity Point and made arrangements to rent it. I was so excited about this house. Until now, Kim and the boys and I had either lived with her parents or a studio apartment. Now, I could afford to provide a really nice home for my family, and I was like a kid in a candy store.

I never moved into it until after the June camp had wrapped up. However, I went throughout the house taking a video so I could show it to Kim, in detail, when I returned home. I will always remember how I felt those first few months of my NFL experience. I was such a proud husband and dad. I had entered a world that, previously, I could only dream about, and now I felt like a king.

After camp, I returned to Nebraska and began packing for the big move to Charlotte. Dan Rose, my father-in-law drove one of our cars and I drove the other with Kim's sister, Cortney, and our Rottweiler. I was full of expectations for the coming year, as we pointed our little caravan eastward, leaving the flat, treeless terrain of Nebraska. We drove all night our first night on the road, and finally stopped in Nashville, Tennessee, the second night, to rest. The hardest part of the trip occurred when we came across the mountains. I had never seen the mountains from the ground and they looked a lot different looming over you, rather than up above, from the window of an airplane. As our caravan wound around the Appalachians then entered the Blue Ridge territory, I admit I was a little nervous. I had a big U-Haul trailer on the back of my Toyota 4Runner. As we traveled, I could feel the pull of the trailer, weaving slightly right and then left, as I cautiously rounded each curve. Thankfully the trip proved uneventful and on the third day, three exhausted travelers finally arrived in Charlotte.

Once we got to Charlotte, I couldn't find the house I had rented. I hadn't been there since I signed the rental contract and I lost all sense of direction concerning where it was located in the subdivision. So Kim's dad took off to try to find it himself. I don't know why he thought he would be able to find it any better than I could, because he hadn't even been to Charlotte before that day. Just as I suspected, Dan got lost. I didn't know where he was and Cortney, by that time, was all excited and freaking out because we couldn't find her dad. I was lost, Dan was lost and Cortney was frantic. It was a real mess. I finally found the street and the house. This occurred before cell phones were common, so we just had to wait on Dan to finally show up, which he eventually did. We unpacked and got the house ready. Kim and her other sister Melissa flew to Charlotte with our two boys the next day. We lived in Prosperity Point for about five months, and then bought a house nearby. Finally, after two years of marriage and two children, we were homeowners.

During the July camp, the coaches decided that I would play as a nickel back, or the backup safety. The starting safeties at the beginning of the 1997 season were Chad Coulter and Pat Terrell. Playing as a nickel back meant that I would only come into the game during a passing situation. Being a competitor, I was not at all satisfied that I was on the second team, and I was determined that before the season ended, I would be a starter.

A preview of what would be a downward trend for the team actually began much earlier at training camp. On the last night of camp quarterback, Kerry Collins, who later admitted his battles with alcoholism, got into a drunken brawl with several other teammates. Collins was accused of using offensive racial slurs against wide receiver, Muhsin Muhammad (Moose) and Norberto Davidds-Garrido, an offensive lineman. A fight ensued, resulting in a punch to Collins' eye from Davidds-Garrido. Several weeks later, in a pre-season game with Denver, Collins was leveled by Denver linebacker, Bill Romanowski and sustained a broken jaw, which removed him from the line-up. Steve Beuerlein took over temporarily while Collins recovered.

Collins went back in as starting quarterback in the third game of the regular season, but was benched after he turned the ball over nine times in two games. Eight of those turnovers were interceptions, and Capers took the brunt of the blame when he announced that he had hurried Collins back into the lineup when he really needed more time to recuperate. Capers could easily have let Collins be the fall guy, but he didn't. He was a players' coach and a stand-up guy. I'll never forget that. As a result, Steve Beuerlein, again took over as quarterback. Carolina was now 2-3 as we went into a bye week, and the future did not look rosy for this season.

Make no mistake about it there was no question that the team was not happy with the way Collins had acted. Being an effective quarterback requires the respect of your teammates. That kind of discord affects the whole team, and it affected what Collins was experiencing mentally. He was a young man, only 24 at the time, who had quarterbacked for Penn State, which went undefeated in 1994. He was also a Heisman Trophy nominee. He was the No.1 pick for Carolina in 1995. His early success with the team led the Carolina Panthers to win the NFC West in 1996 and a Pro Bowl berth for himself. The pressure was tremendous for him to perform even better in 1997. All this was happening to him, yet he was only two years out of college. After an unbelievable year of riding a high note, he made a drunken statement and his world came crashing down. In spite of the fact that Collins apologized to those involved and the team in general, the writing was on the wall for him at Carolina. Fans sat (and stood) angrily in the stands that year, watching this discord in the team play out over and over, until Collins had finally had enough.

As for my exposure to what was happening with the team, I didn't see a lot of what was going on as a rookie. I was so focused on doing my best for the team and becoming a starter that I didn't really pay a lot of attention to some of the off-field talk that was developing over Collins. I just wanted to make an impact on this football team. My philosophy has always been to only worry about what I can control, and at that time it equated to the effort that I put into playing the game to my highest potential..

We were preparing to play the Minnesota Vikings the following Sunday. I came in on Wednesday, which was the first day of practice during game week.

George Catavolis, my position coach, stopped me and said, "I need to talk with you."

I thought, man, what's going on? I was nervous and all sorts of scenarios were running through my head. I was wondering, do I still have a job? Am I cut? I didn't know what to expect. We walked in the office and I saw that Eric Davis was there. There were just the three of us, as I waited to find out the reason why I had been summoned.

Capers looked at me and said, "We're going to start you this week." There was total silence in the room.

In my mind I thought, that's what I'm talking about! Yeah, I'm ready! I was both nervous and excited at the same time. Then I looked at him and said as coolly as my emotions would allow, "Okay."

"You think you can do it?" Capers asked.

"Yeah," I replied.

Davis looked at me with an expression on his face that said, okay young fella, we're going to be counting on you. You've got to step up the game. This is for real. At the same time, though, I think he believed that I was ready to start.

Right there in that room I had so much confidence. I knew the coach thought I was ready, and I was convinced that Eric Davis, the guy I looked up to more than any other on the team thought so, too. From that point on, I started in almost every game I played until the day I retired in 2007.

I was bursting with so much excitement that I could not wait to get out of that place and to go home and tell Kim about the news. I knew, above anyone else, that she would be as proud and happy as I was, about what this milestone meant in my career. When I finally arrived home, I tried to keep my emotions in check as I came in the house. Michael ran up to me and gave me a big hug.

"Daddy! Daddy! You're home." He shouted as he ran towards me.

I picked him up, hugged him and gave him a kiss.

"What have you been doing today with Mommy?" I asked him.

Isaiah had heard Michael and wandered into the room. I lifted him up and gave him his kiss. Then, last but not least I finally went over to Kim, who stood expectantly waiting to hear about my day. I was bursting with the news and the expression on my face told her that something had happened.

"Guess what happened at work, today? I teased.

My expression and the tone of the question must have sounded as if something was wrong, so Kim thought something bad had happened.

"What?" Kim asked hesitantly, not sure that the answer would be to her liking.

"Well, Mrs. Minter," I began "your husband is going to be the new starting free safety for the Carolina Panthers this next game."

Kim and I both started crying and hugging each other. It was so great to have this moment to share together. Especially since Kim had been with me through so many of the disappointing times.

Then she stood back for a second and asked hesitantly, "whose spot will you be taking in the starting lineup?"

My expression changed from a big smile to a grimace.

"Pat Terrell," I said solemnly.

That is always the difficult part of playing sports because my family and Pat's family were friends. Kim was even in a Bible study with Pat's wife. So it was a bitter sweet moment. The one thing that I am always thankful for is how Pat never let that ever change our relationship. He understood the big picture which is that football is a business and not personal.

I had achieved my goal of making it to the NFL and I was learning so much. I tried not to dwell on the idea that the Panthers were having a losing season, or the fact that when Collins returned to the game he continued his downward spiral of interceptions. Even the defense was not playing very well. I told myself that maybe it was because of the inordinate number of injuries we had. I was caught up in trying to let Mike Minter get his job done.

Then, around the 10th game, I hit what is called the "rookie wall." I couldn't run. I was so tired and beaten up, I could hardly move. My legs felt so heavy. Part of the reason was the difference between the NFL and college football. By the end of November, in college, you're done with the regular season and you have several weeks to prepare for the championship games. Unlike collegiate football, in the NFL the regular season continues throughout December. That five-to-six game stretch at the end of my first NFL year was very tough for me.

In spite of the fact that my rookie year was not as spectacular as I had envisioned, I can say that there were a few memorable moments. I am especially pleased to have been a part of Sam Mills last year as a player.

I used to sit and watch Sam to see how he conducted himself both on and off the field. I wanted to see what he did to prepare himself for a game. Football was everything to Sam. It was Sam who taught me the importance of gaining the respect of the veterans on the team. The first time he came up to me and said,

"You're going to be all right," I knew I had arrived. And he and I used to have a running joke about who was the tallest, because Sam Mills was a short guy too.

I will always remember listening to Sam as he addressed the team before the final game of his playing career. He was so emotional and I kept thinking that I wanted to get out there and win this game for him. Sam was a quiet man, especially with the rookies, but he was a strong leader on the team, and he could hit.

I remember one time we were in a game and I was about to tackle the running back, but Sam got there first. Sam hit him so hard that it sounded like a car wreck, and I actually stopped and said, "Wow! That was a hit!"

One other memorable game with Sam was in that same season, against the Saint Louis Rams. It was the fourth down with only two minutes left in the game. We had the game won if we could just hold them. The Rams quarterback, Tony Banks, fired a pass to Ernie Conwell, who was Sam's man to cover. Conwell got away from him, pulled in the pass, and was running down the field for a touchdown. Sam was chasing him down the field but he couldn't catch him. I saw what was happening and chased Conwell down to the four-yard line and was able to make a touchdown-saving tackle. If they had scored they would have won, but we prevailed this time and came away with a 16-10 win.

Afterwards, Sam came up to me and said, "I appreciate you helping me out, young fella. I needed your help on that one." He talked about that play with me every year, even after he retired as a player and joined the team as a defensive coach.

I initially thought that I was just doing my job, although I appreciated that a veteran, especially one I admired so much, would make a big deal about it. Now that I have retired, however, I understand what he was going through. People were saying that he was getting too old to run and had lost his step. If we had been beaten in that game because Sam had allowed the guy to score, I know it would have eaten at him. To be a professional athlete in any sport, you have to have a lot of pride in what you do, and when you fail to do your job and let your teammates down, it's the worst feeling in the world.

Another memorable moment was on Fan Appreciation Day that year. Dom

Capers had the team scrimmage for the fans. On one particular play, Scott Green caught the ball and I hit him so hard that the ball came out and he flew up in the air. Sam saw it happen and said, talking about me, "We've got a player here." He liked to talk to me about that play also.

At this point in my rookie season, our record stood at 7-8 and we were set to play the Rams in the last game of our regular season. We felt confident going into the game because Carolina had beaten the Rams earlier in the season. We were finishing up the home-and-home series, and I wanted to win this game so much for Sam. Also, the team could end the season at 8-8. It was important to me. It wasn't a winning season, but not a losing one either, and it still left the possibility of making the playoffs.

Even now, I do not understand what happened that day. It was the first time I can remember seeing teammates quit mentally and physically. In spite of the fact that we had had no chance to win the conference title that year, we still had an opportunity to make the playoffs as a wild card team, but the team just gave up. It was one of the first times that I saw what the NFL was really all about. I saw the reality of how some people act in this league. The truth is that there are some guys who just shut down once they realize they aren't going to the playoffs. They start thinking about other things when they are on the field. Apparently, their minds were on traveling and going home, not finishing the game. It was the first time that I had ever been on a football team that didn't give 110% on the field, and it shocked me. From elementary school through college, I had always been on teams that played hard whether they won or lost. To be out there on the field and see in the players' eyes that they didn't want to be out there, just blew my mind.

We lost that game 30-18 and, as I watched Sam Mills leave the field, crying and waving to the fans, it was tough to swallow. I have never understood why some of those players did not have any pride in trying to win that game, if for no other reason than to honor Sam in his farewell game.

Sam Mills loved football and was good at it. Even after he came back in as a scout, I saw the kind of relationships he built. Later, he returned from retirement to join the Panthers as a defensive coach. He was young by usual coaching standards, but I saw the growth of him as a teacher and mentor. I saw how he was able to explain to other players what he wanted them to learn. Coaches break down different segments of the game in order to show you how to react to particular circumstances. Sam Mills, however, would break down every play, such as third down and five or third down and nine. I remember he had about 50 plays going back as much as five years just for third down and goal. I had a great relationship with Sam.

Although we ended the season 7-9, we were still second in the NFC West. We lost the division that year to the San Francisco 49ers. Nevertheless, I have heard it said that second place is just the first loser. It was a very disillusioning time to realize that in all my years of football, I had never played on any team that had a losing season. It was certainly something that I never anticipated so early in my career.

The interim period between the end of the 1997 season and the beginning of training for 1998 was especially hard on me. Being on a losing team affected me, but in addition, I was now faced with months of time on my hands. In college there is never any spare time. You are going to school and playing football. In your senior year, after the football season you are preparing for the Senior Bowl, the Combine and then pro days, which lead up to the draft in April. That was the first time in my entire life that I had absolutely nothing to do and it was driving me crazy. Kim and I finally took the boys and travelled, spending a lot of time visiting our families. It is something Kim misses now that I have retired and have become involved more in business and the community. I am also more involved in my church, and as the children get older many activities are the results of what they are doing. Now, I don't have the time I used to have, but back then, the idleness during January to March 1998, was an unfamiliar experience for me.

It was during this time Kim and I began to notice that Isaiah, who was now one year old, had developed a breathing problem. It was so gradual that at first we did not think much about it. But, as the year progressed from 1997 to 1998, his breathing became more and more labored. His pediatrician, during his check-ups did not even realize that a problem was slowly developing that could have eventually cost him his life.

Finally, on one doctor's visit, he informed us, "Something is definitely restricting his air passage, let's run some tests."

Kim and I began to worry at this point. Maybe we should have realized sooner that Isaiah was ill. We waited impatiently as each test brought back inconclusive results. Finally, the doctors found the cause. It was a long cyst that was growing against his trachea and with each passing month it pressed against his airway threatening to completely cut off his breathing.

I remember holding him as I sat in the hospital. "God, I know have to put Isaiah in Your hands, but You know how hard it is for me. You gave him to Kim and me, and Isaiah has been such a blessing to us. "Please God," I pleaded. "Let us keep him a little longer." Afterwards, when the operation was over and the doctor told us he would have a complete recovery, I was so relieved.

There had been so much turmoil this past year. First I was tense about being drafted. Then, I experienced a losing season during my first year of professional football. Now, we faced Isaiah's illness. It had definitely been a rough road. Wasn't life was suppose to be easy now that I had made it to the NFL? Wrong! I found out early, in my own personal experience, that money won't solve all your problems and it can't stop problems from coming. Only God, can only give you peace that gets you to the other side when things don't go your way.

I remember heading into the new season of 1998 and that I felt pretty good about the team. During the past season the Panthers had been hit with a lot of injuries. Now, I thought, we have Kevin Greene back on the team. He had left the team the previous year due to a contract dispute. I felt confident that our defense was going to be like the 1996 team all over again. I assumed that although Kerry Collins had come off with a disappointing year in 1997, he would rebound effectively. In fact, most of the team thought our offense would do well that upcoming season. The coaches had decided to bring back to some of the 1996 players. Besides Kevin Greene, Troy Cook had come back to play with the defense. I think they were reaching back to 1996 to see if the team could recoup some of its former magic. However, we lost the first two games of the season and had an early bye week. That spark of glory had not materialized, as anticipated.

At that time I had a piece of cartilage floating around in my knee and it began to hurt. We were going to play Green Bay after the bye week, so the team physician decided this would be the opportune time to have it scoped and cleaned out. I didn't think it was going to be a big deal. I would go in on Monday, have the procedure and be ready to play by the next weekend. However, I woke up on Tuesday and there was blood everywhere in my bandages. I didn't really think very much about it and I went in to rehab, but blood kept seeping out while I was doing my exercises.

Rehab after surgery consisted of contracting the muscles in my thighs to strengthen them, without using weights. That's all I was doing, yet it was causing my knee to bleed. At that point the trainers became concerned and said I needed to get into the doctor to see what was going on. On Wednesday, I went into the doctor, who said I was working too hard and I needed to slow down. I was concerned because I knew I had to get ready for the game with Green Bay the following week. The doctor discussed giving me antibiotics but decided I should be fine without them. That was fine with me, because I didn't want to have any reason that would keep me from playing at my best, in the upcoming game. I continued to rehab on Thursday and Friday for the game. I could walk and run so I thought everything was going to be fine for the game the next week. Then, on Saturday of our bye week, we were off and I was home. I took a nap, but when I got up and got out of the bed my knee was stiff. I wondered why my knee was so stiff but I convinced myself that it was because of the surgery, in addition to the fact that I had been working out. I thought it would loosen up and go away, but as the day progressed, it started getting worse and then began swelling.

Finally, Kim said, "You need to call the trainer and go to the doctor and see what's wrong with your knee."

I sloughed it off and said to her, "This stuff happens all the time. It's going to be all right."

That night, however, I was sweating one minute and cold and shivering the next. Kim saw that I was really sick and said to me, "I don't care what you say I'm calling the trainer now!"

I finally relented. "Okay, I'll call."

I got in touch with the trainer and he said "Mike, we've got to get you to the hospital right now!"

We had some friends, Tony and Brook Villa, visiting with us. So it was decided that Tony would drive me to the hospital. By that time, my leg hurt so bad that you couldn't even touch it and if we went over any bumps on the road it felt like needles and hammering going through my whole body. By the time I reached the hospital I was delirious. As soon as we arrived, nurses began to administer a painkiller. To make a bad situation worse, however, the painkillers caused a allergic reaction and I started itching all over my body. I was delirious, in pain, and itching all over. I ended up in Emergency for about 12 hours, while they pumped antibiotics in me trying to get that infection out of me so they could finally operate. After the surgery, I ended up staying in the hospital about a week and a half or two weeks. Later I found out I almost died from a staph infection.

One interesting aspect of the ordeal was that during my stay at the hospital, Jerry Richardson, owner of the Carolina Panthers, came to my room to see me. It was the first time I'd really gotten an opportunity to meet him on a personal level. I thought that it was cool that the owner of the Panthers came to see a player. Through his actions I saw that his players meant something to him. Perhaps it was because, in years past, he also had been a player, with the Baltimore Colts. Regardless, it was the beginning of a connection that I still have with him. It really meant something significant to me that he took the time to come and see me.

While I was in the hospital I lost about 30 pounds. When I left, I only weighed about 160 or 165, so I really looked sick. When I went to the stadium I looked so sick and my face was all drawn. Players were coming up to me to tell me they were worried and had been praying for me. I looked so bad that the coaches were trying to decide if they were going to put me on injured reserve status. That was a big deal to me. They even suggested that I have some kind of surgery where they pick your bones.

I called my doctor in Nebraska who had originally done my ACL surgery to ask him about it. He said, "Mike, don't do it. It's not perfected yet, but need to go on IR. You shouldn't be playing with a staph infection." I said "okay" and I listened to him about the surgery but I didn't listen to him about going on IR.

I missed ten games that season while I was recovering. I remember during that time that Mr. Richardson and I had a conversation. Mr. Richardson said to me, "Young fella, you get back on that field."

I took his comments seriously and thought, hey, I better get back on that field. I worked hard rehabbing and training and I finally got to play during the last four games of the season. The first game that I was back, we were playing the San Francisco 49'ers. In order to ease me back into the action and not wear me out, I didn't start that game or the next one with Washington. Those games I only came in during third down passing situations.

The next to last game with the St. Louis Rams, I started. As I recall, it was the end of the game, and they were trying to score, but I intercepted the ball on the sidelines and ran out of bounds, sealing the win. I was so excited. It was the first interception of my NFL career and it couldn't have come at a better time. In fact the whole team and coaches were excited.

I remember Eric Davis came to me and said, "I was starting to get worried about you son. I was questioning if you could play football, because you hadn't made a big play, but now I know you can do it." He was always teasing me.

Our last game was against the Colts, I could hardly walk because my knee hurt so badly from playing so hard on the field. I guess I should have listened to my doctor in Nebraska and gone on injured reserve. I did a lot of damage to my knee that year, and it almost ended my career.

During the time that I wasn't in the game, I sat on the sidelines. It was then that I really began to see the debacle of a team falling apart. First, Kerry Collins played only four games, all of which we lost. Before the season was even over, he was waived and allowed to leave Carolina and finish the year with the New Orleans Saints.

One particular game I remember, I was on the sitting on bench and we weren't playing very well. Defensive linebackers' coach, Kevin Steele, was upset and mad about how the defense was playing and he got in Kevin Greene's face about it. He said something harsh to Kevin Greene.

Greene said to him, "Man, you better get out of my face."

To which Steele replied, "I'm going nowhere. You don't scare me!"

All of a sudden Kevin Greene picked Steele up by his jacket collar and was choking him. Both of them were heated and it just blew my mind that a player would do something like that to a coach. I had never seen anything like that before.

The reality of it all began to sink in. We had released a perfectly healthy starting quarterback at midseason because he'd "lost his passion for the game." We had played poorly for most of the season. And now, I had just witnessed one of our defensive leaders and a coach getting into a big time physical confrontation. There was no longer any doubt in my mind. We had just lost the team.

Then there was Fred Lane. Fred had come to the Panthers during the 1997 season as an undrafted free agent. He had captured the preseason attention of the Carolina fans that year by the heart and energy he put into the game. Fans waited expectantly to see if Lane would make the pre-season cut that year and he survived to make the opening day roster. In fact, in spite of some mediocre performances turned in by many of the seasoned players, he was the team leader with 809 rushing yards that year, which included seven touchdowns. During the 1998 season, Lane again led the team, with 717 rushing yards, and 5 touchdowns. But for all the good things he brought to the game, he brought about a negative reaction from Mr. Richardson. When he would score a touchdown, Lane would usually go to the opposing team and make obscene gestures. He was also well known after scoring a touchdown, for entertaining the fans with his famous "worm" imitation in the end zone. Like Vince Lombardi of the 1960's Green Bay packers, Mr. Richardson is about excellence and respect. He isn't fond of players who act that brashly on the field in full view of the public. So, to a certain extent, Lane's antics created a negative image for himself and for the team.

The last four games that year, the team knew we were playing for the coaches' jobs. We all stepped up and started playing some good football. By the end of the season, the coaches had us practicing in full pads. In fact, even the injured people had to put on full pads. I don't know why. If I had to make a judgment it was because they were in a tight situation. They knew their jobs were on the line and they panicked. Instead of working smarter they must have thought if we just worked harder it would make everything better. They didn't understand that it wasn't that we weren't playing hard. It was a chemistry thing. We had lost it and we were all going in different directions. It wasn't because we didn't work hard.

Personally, I didn't want Dom Capers to get fired. As a team, we liked him. We were mad when we realized that he was in jeopardy of losing his job. He was a players' coach. You could talk to him and he was very accessible. You knew that he cared about you as a player. Those are rare qualities in a lot of coaches that occupy the top jobs in the NFL.

After the season ended, the team was all gathered together for the final meeting to discuss team issues. Dom came in and started talking about the season.

Dom said, "We ended up 4-12 and when you end up 4-12 you get a new coach in this league and that's what's happened. You're going to have a new coach."

As a second year player, I was mad and sad because I felt close to Dom Capers. Many of the other players felt the same way. In that meeting some guys stood up and booed and hollered, but it wasn't going to change anything. Dom Capers walked out and away from the Carolina Panthers and the 1998 season, which, in my opinion, ended far worse then it had begun. We finished 4-12 leaving us third in the NFC West division standings, with only the St Louis Rams below us in last place.

Chapter 7

THE GEORGE SEIFERT YEARS 1999-2001

Silence may be golden...but
words of encouragement fetch a far greater price.

We knew, of course, we were getting a new coach, but the team had no idea who the coach was going to be until late in the off-season of 1999. We heard George Seifert's name being rumored, but Seifert was getting thrown into just about every NFL head coaching vacancy, so the team wasn't sure whether he was really being considered or not.

I was sure that Mr. Richardson was going to go get the person he wanted, whoever he turned out to be. When Mr. Richardson is forced to make a move, you'd better believe he's going to make the best move for the team. He was going to go get his man and George Seifert was his man back then, and he got him. Mr. Richardson wants to win. He understands what it takes to win and he's willing to pay his coaches and pay his players to win. That's why I love him so much, because he's a 'go getter' and a winner. He wants to win the Super Bowl. The determination that was in his face always made me want to be around him.

When we heard that George Seifert was going to be the coach I was excited, along with the rest of the team. Seifert had won two Super Bowls when he coached the San Francisco 49'ers. I talked to Eric Davis about him because Davis had played for him at San Francisco, so I kind of got to know a little bit about him from our conversations. In general the team thought hiring Seifert was a good move, and we were anxious to get started preparing for the new season.

When Coach Seifert arrived he called me into his office and said to me, "Mike, I heard you play safety. Is that right?"

"Yes sir, I can play," I said.

Seifert replied, "Good, good. I asked my safeties to cover, and I hear you can cover the slot real well."

"Yeah," I said. "We'll see what we can do."

Seifert replied, "Okay then. I look forward to working with you."

That's how we started off our relationship together and it was just about the only conversation we ever had one-on-one.

The switch to Seifert from Capers brought a lot more than a change in coaches. With Dom Capers, we used a West Coast Defense. With Seifert our defense changed from 3-4 to 4-3. In the 3-4 defense, the strong safety typically sets up closer to the line of scrimmage, so he basically acts as a fourth linebacker. Meanwhile, the free safety is usually in the middle of the field. Honestly, when we switched defense to 4-3 it was easier for me. In the 4-3 with a cover scheme four or cover two scheme, they interchange. The strong safety will generally line up to the strong side of the opposing team's formation, which is the side that the tight end sets up on. The free safety will line up to the weaker side of the formation. I had never played a 3-4 defense, before I came to the Panthers. I played 4-3 in college. For me, the 3-4 defense was more complicated and I had to learn it. So I was cool with the change because the 4-3 defense was easier to understand.

That year, we lost Chad Coulter and I moved from free safety to strong safety. As a result of my move, the coaching staff moved Brent Alexander into free safety. When Seifert came in, Brent Alexander and Doug Evans, who had been picked up in 1998, remained as free safeties. The Panthers released Tyrone Poole, but we still had Eric Davis, so the 1999 team consisted of Eric Davis, Brent Alexander, Doug Evans and myself, who filled the four starting secondary slots.

From a football standpoint, the biggest difference I saw between Dom

Capers and George Seifert was that Dom Capers was more of a grinder. He wanted a physical team. On the other hand, Seifert preferred more finesse, west coast style. With Seifert, practice wasn't as hard, but that's not always a good thing. During practice, we couldn't hit a receiver and we didn't practice in pads. With Capers, you could hit a receiver. The Capers philosophy was all about defense. Seifert was all about offense.

I also remember that Capers was a hard worker. Sometimes he would even sleep at the stadium. Seifert wasn't as hard working and the team could tell. With Seifert as coach the Carolina Panthers never had a winning season.

Our 1999 season began with enthusiasm. In that year's draft, Carolina had chosen Chris Terry an offensive tackle from Georgia and Mike Rucker a defensive end, and one of my old teammates from Nebraska. In addition, we picked up Hannibal Navies, a lineman out of Colorado. Terry was eventually released by Carolina in 2002. Navies later played for the Green Bay Packers, then the Cincinnati Bengals before settling with the San Francisco 49ers. Rucker was destined for a longer run at Carolina.

I knew Ruck from school. He had been a sophomore when I was a senior at Nebraska. I like to tease him, telling him that at school, he was such a clown that I wasn't sure he would make it in football. I thought he didn't work hard enough, and he was always joking, never taking anything seriously. It wasn't true, but I like to joke with him about it. I told him that I remember watching him in his last game of the season for Nebraska, and then in the 1999 Senior Bowl. He dominated those games, and I wondered where along the line he got so good. Then the Panthers drafted him. In fact I was one of the reasons he came to Carolina. The coaches had asked me what I thought about him and I said he would be a good addition to the team. Of course he doesn't like it very much when I remind him that he owes me.

After Ruck came to the Panthers, I tried to help him out and he began to hang around the other Nebraska players who were now with Carolina. Jason Peter was another former Husker defensive lineman who was also on the team at that time.

Eventually, Ruck and I began to develop a relationship and really got close when he was ready to sign his second contract. We even moved into the same neighborhood and his wife, Kristina, who is also from Nebraska, became close friends with Kim.

Ruck also began to grow spiritually and began taking that aspect of his life much more seriously. During this time, Moose also became a Christian. One day the three of us, along with former Panther, Stephen Davis, were all talking about daycare for our kids. We were all concerned that there didn't appear to be any daycare and learning environments in our area that had a faith-based philosophy or curriculum. Ultimately, we decided to start our own, and that's how Ruckus House got started. It was not named for Mike Rucker, but he came up with the name because the word "ruckus" indicates a place where kids can kick back and have fun. I believe the combination of all these factors are what made us all the close friends we are today.

Having a long relationship like I have had with Moose and Ruck is not nearly as common in the NFL as it was before the days of free agency. Today, guys get cut or their contracts expire, and they move to other teams. Unlike the old days of NFL football, there aren't as many teams that stay together. If you look at some of the more dominant teams that were around before free agency, you'll find a number of guys that remained life long friends because they played so long together. These were teams like the San Francisco 49ers, the Dallas Cowboys and the Buffalo Bills, who were together for five to ten years. That was especially true with the core guys on the team. Because it isn't as common as in the past, it is especially nice for me to have the opportunity to develop and grow along with friends such as Moose and Ruck.

Our first game that season was with New Orleans, and we were fired up and hopeful that the season would end with a trip to the Super Bowl, but we lost 19-10. Our next game also ended with a loss, 20-22 against the Jacksonville Jaguars. By this time Fred Lane, whose rushing performances during the past two seasons had set a team record, had been suspended by the Panthers for what were called off-field issues. He was traded to the Indianapolis Colts after the season ended but would never play football again. In July, 2000 he was indicted on drug charges by a Tennessee grand jury, and only a few days later, he was shot and killed by his estranged wife.

Lane had been replaced in the starting lineup by running back Tshimanga Biakabatuka, as the Panthers faced off against the Washington Redskins on October 3, 1999. Biakabatuka had played well in the previous week's game against the Cincinnati Bengals, and that game had been our first win of the season. The game with Washington started well for us with Carolina scoring three touchdowns. Biakabatuka had run 60 and 45 yards respectively to score two of those touchdowns in the first quarter. We had built a 21-0 lead, and a field goal increased it to 24-0. Seifert, who was known for rotating running backs, took Biakabatuka out of the game...a decision that would change the whole momentum of the game.

Washington rallied, and by the fourth quarter they had racked up a 35-24 lead over us. With less than eight minutes remaining in the game Carolina drew closer once more with Steve Beuerlein's touchdown pass to Wesley Walls making the score 30-35. Then Biakabatuka, who had come back into the game, ran for his third touchdown that day, putting Carolina in front 36-35. We had missed the extra point on both scores, but it still looked good for us. The momentum had shifted our way once more. With only four minutes left in the game, we were holding on with a vengeance, but our offense was held on downs, so we punted the ball and it was fumbled on the Redskin 19 yard line. We recovered it, but Washington's coach, Norv Turner challenged the call and it was reversed. The Redskins took that opportunity to put together a 69-yard drive that would put them within field goal range at the 31-yard line. With only six seconds remaining Washington kicked a field goal to make the final score 38-36. It was a bitter, heartbreaking loss and the kind that would come back to haunt the Panthers over the next few years. The Washington game would be destined to be repeated over and over and reach its zenith in 2001 when we developed a reputation as a team for racking up a large lead then losing the game in the last two minutes of play.

After the Washington game, Seifert was so mad that he called all the defensive backs together and said, "Let me tell you something. If I could fire all you guys, I would, but I can't because I don't have any replacements for you, so you're lucky." Seifert woke me up. It was the first time that a coach had ever come to me and said, you're going to get cut. It was a wakeup call for all of us.

Our season rocked along. We would win the next game with the San Francisco 49er's and then lose the following two games. By November 1, 1999, we had won a total of three games during the 10 weeks of the season. It appeared that we were headed in the same direction as our record during previous year.

Then in mid-November, the Carolina Panthers would become known throughout as the first NFL team ever to have an active player accused of murder. It was not the attention the team needed or wanted.

Rae Carruth and I, born only five days apart were rookies together. Both of us had both been drafted in 1997. Carruth was picked 27th overall and had signed a four year $3.7 million contract. He still had one more year left on it when he was accused in mid-November of participating in the shooting of his pregnant girlfriend.

Rae grew up in Sacramento, California in a neighborhood filled with drugs and crime. He escaped that fate through football just as many athletes have. He went on to play for the University of Colorado where he excelled as a wide receiver. With his selection by the Carolina Panthers, his life had changed overnight.. Very soon after his admittance into the world of the NFL, Carruth's income was no longer sufficient to cover his obligations. Bad investments, and lawsuits against him for breach of contract, threatened to extinguish the lifestyle he had worked so hard to achieve.

Soon after the start of the 1998 season Carruth had broken his ankle, which put him out for the year. He played six games during the 1999 season before he sprained his ankle, taking him out of the game once more. He was considered a liability to the team due to his high salary, and his off-field problems were growing almost as fast as his debt. Then, his pregnant girlfriend was shot, but before she lapsed into a comma she implicated him in the crime. The child, a son, who was determined to be Carruth's, was born several weeks prematurely in November 1999, and with cerebral palsy, due to the distress that the baby endured at birth. Carruth's girlfriend, Cherica Adams died in December of that year. A few days later, the Carolina Panthers released Carruth and early in January, 2000, he was indicted for murder.

One of the biggest challenges a coach in the NFL has when adversity strikes a team, is how to minimize the distraction, or even use it as motivational tool. If a coach can figure that out he can be a great coach in the NFL.

On a more positive note, an exciting event regarding my life did occur in mid November, 1999 when the Panthers played the Cleveland Browns in Cleveland. The game was scheduled for November 21st so before we left to fly there, I decided to call Mama and ask her for information on how to contact my dad's family. I was able to locate them and told them when I was arriving and where the team would be staying.

My grandmother, Goldine Minter, came to the hotel along with my Aunt Nancy Minter, on my dad's side. My grandfather had passed away years before. I had so many questions I wanted to ask them. My grandmother, who was a very small women hugged me and said, "I can't believe my baby is out on that football field playing. They better not be hurting you."

I laughed and said, "No ma'am they aren't hurting me." She had brought a picture of my dad and me when I was just a baby. He looked just like me. She also told me my dad was a great dancer and he was a disk jockey. She asked if I could dance but I had to tell her no.

It was a strange feeling to be standing in front of my grandmother, who I had never met before. There stood my dad's own mother. In just a few seconds a whole range of emotions overwhelmed me. I wanted to laugh and cry at the same time. Yet I also felt sadness. Part of me wished that I was still a little boy, able to enjoy the spoiling that only a grandmother can give her grandchildren. I wanted to really get to know this woman, who had been so much a part of my dad's life. But I knew the time had passed for that to happen with any consistency. Other than a few occasional visits or telephone conversations, our interaction would be limited. Life and time had marched on for both of us and left in its wake a void that would never be completely filled.

This was the first contact I'd had with my dad's family in 30 years. Other than an incident that happened during the time I was waiting to be drafted, it was the only real information I had on my dad's family. It happened in 1997, during the period between the Combine and the draft. I flew to meet Bill Parcells, head coach of the New York Jets. As I waited in Coach Parcells' office, one of the secretaries there noticed my name and said to me, "I knew a Mike Minter when I was growing up in Cleveland." I said, "Wow, that's where I'm from. He was my daddy."

The woman replied, "I knew him very well. In fact, we went to catholic school and Julliard High School together. He was a great athlete and you look just like him. She told me a lot about my dad and his childhood. I thought, man, this is too much! The interesting thing about that whole visit was that I never got to meet with Coach Parcells. I believe now that the whole purpose of my visit was to find out about my dad.

We won the game with Cleveland that year, 31-17 and returned home. Surprisingly, from November through December our win-loss record actually improved. We finished the last half of the 1999 season with an additional five wins and only three losses. It was a phenomenal achievement considering what had been taking place with the team. We ended the season second in the NFC West but lost out on the wildcard berth due to a tie breaker rule that said the winner would be the team that had scored the most points during the season. Even though when we played the New Orleans Saints and won with an impressive 45-13 victory, it was still not enough to outscore our competition, the Green Bay Packers that year. We ended the season 8-8. It wasn't an impressive record but it was a definite improvement over the past year's record of 4-12.

I also realized, after the 2000 season I would become a free agent. However, I didn't want to be a potential candidate who was cut from the lineup. That would certainly affect any bargaining power I had with the Panthers or any other team. So I watched the draft carefully that April and saw that Seifert had drafted two defensive backs, Rashard Anderson and Deon Grant. These guys were drafted in the first and second rounds so I knew that Seifert was serious about having them play. I was convinced that Brent Alexander and I were in trouble. Then during summer camp the Panthers let Brent go.

Before he left, Brent came to me and said, "I asked Seifert what he was going to do about you, but he said he didn't know."

I said to Brent, "Okay." Now, I'm not a person who seeks out confrontation, but this time, there wasn't much I could do about this situation except to approach it head on. I knew I was in jeopardy of losing my job! So I simply took the bull by the horns, so to speak, and went directly to Coach Seifert's office.

I said to him, "I'm ready to compete with anyone you bring in here. What I want to know is whether or not it's going to be fair. I don't care who you bring in here. If it's fair and it's on the field, I'll beat anyone that you bring in here, but I've got to know that it's going to be a fair competition." Seifert had been Coach of the Panthers for an entire year and this was only the second conversation we had together.

Seifert said to me, "Mike, it's going to be fair. The best man's going to win."

"Well, that's all I can ask," I replied, "If I know it's fair, I know I'll be on the field."

I knew I had to confront Seifert about this because when I first came to this team Eric Davis had said to me, "Mike, in this league jobs are not won or lost they're given and taken." So that was on my mind when I saw it happening to me. If he was considering someone else for my job, I knew I had to go talk to him.

I went to training camp and probably prayed the hardest I can remember. I asked for the Lord to show me direction and show me where I was going with my life. He took me to the book of Psalms in the Bible, and I read Psalms each morning before I went to practice. Through this experience, God showed me in His Word that I can't trust in man. I can't trust in football. I can only trust in Him. He is my source and I needed to get my strength from Him. It was an amazing revelation.

In the NFL if the coach is getting ready to make a move to replace a safety, he'll put the new player in on third down during practices and in the preseason games. They put the player in on third down because he isn't required to think as much, since the odds are that this is a passing down. It gives him some exposure and the coach gets a chance to see him play. They don't put them in on first or second down because those downs can be running or passing situations and you need some experience for that. So during training camp the coach started putting Anderson and Grant in on third down situations.

One day at practice I was watching the coach do this, and I was getting madder and madder. I finally decided that the next time the coach tried to replace me; I would not come off that field. We had just gotten done practicing first and second down reps and were ready for third downs', and one of those new draftees started to run onto the field.

I waved him off and said, "I've got it."

The defensive coordinator had sent him in, so the guy looked at me kind of funny like he was asking what am I supposed to do here? He was getting ready to run back to the sideline and John Marshall, defensive coordinator stopped practice.

Marshall came over to me and said, "Mike, what are you doing?"

I told him, "Man, I've got this. I can play. I've got this."

Marshall said to me, "Well, you know that these guys are the starting safeties on third down."

"Don't worry, I've got it," I shot back.

So we were talking back and forth like that and Coach Seifert walked towards us and asked, "What's going on?"

I said to Seifert, "I've got this Coach."

Then Marshall interjected, "Mike what are you doing?"

But Seifert said to Marshall, "Leave him alone. I like that."

I could not believe that the head coach did not kick me out of practice, and I even surprised myself in the way that I talked him. It was so uncharacteristic of me. But I felt that the job I worked so hard for was being threatened. I had been put in a position where I was forced to show the coach that I was confident in what I could do. I was convinced that I had to prove to him that he couldn't take my niceness for weakness.

At this point I was thinking to myself. Is that what you want? Well, let's go then. So I didn't come off the field. Two or three practices later Deon Grant severely hurt his hip in practice, which put him out for the season.

As we came into the regular season, the coaches were coming to the conclusion that Rashard Anderson was not going to be able to play the way they had anticipated. So the coaches brought in Eugene Robinson to take his place. We also picked up Eric Swann. I think the team philosophy back then was to sign all these older players from past years in the hope that the team would exhibit some of that magic from the 1996 season. Reggie White and Eugene Robinson came to practice the last week of training camp that year, only a few weeks before the season started.

The week of the first preseason game we were practicing and George Seifert came into the huddle. Someone said to him "Hey, coach, you better watch Mike Minter."

I hollered back "You don't need to watch me, I've got this." I knew he was referring to the Washington game during the past season when we got toasted.

Then someone else said, "Don't let Mike Minter run up to that line of scrimmage while they're throwing the ball over his head."

I snapped back, in response, "Coach you don't need to worry about me. I've got this. I'm all right."

We started practicing but Rashard Anderson messed up. So we went back into a huddle and Seifert called Eugene Robinson over and said, "Robinson get in here. Rashard you get out." That was the end of Rashhard Anderson.

Eugene Robinson came in and started as the other safety with me that year. For the past two years I had started with Brent Alexander and now he was gone. It's difficult with someone new because you have to learn to play together and get in sync. Robinson had just come in and we had not even had time in training camp to play together. I have to say, though, that I really enjoyed playing with him. Eugene had been through so much and had so much experience playing safety that I was able to learn a lot of nuances of the game. Chad Coulter, who I had played with my first year, was young and so was Brent Alexander. The difference was that Robinson was the first guy I played with who had made it to the Super Bowl and had played in the Pro Bowl. I learned a lot from him that year.

The 2000 season was once more uneventful for the Panthers. The last game of the season was in Oakland with the Raiders and they pounded us 52-9. At the beginning of the game, it didn't appear that it would be that disastrous for us. With only eight minutes left in the first quarter Oakland scored a touchdown, but we answered two minutes later with a field goal. Then, just into second quarter Oakland scored a field goal, making the score 10-3. However, we answered with two more field goals, but Oakland continued to score touchdowns, making the score 24-9 at halftime.

During the second half I'm not even sure the Panther's team showed up on the field, because Oakland proceeded to score an additional 28 points while the Panthers were unable to answer at all. That year, we ended up 7-9, the same record we had during my very first year in the NFL.

The fourth year of my contract was up and I was now a free agent. I could have left the Panthers and played with any NFL team that wanted me, but my heart was still to stay with Carolina, if they would pay me what I believed I was worth.

This was my first contract since I originally signed with the Panthers, and, for most NFL players, it means their first really big payday. Now I suppose there are many people who think that football players are way overpaid. That may be the case, but to offset that position, the element of physical risk each player assumes when he takes the field must be factored into the equation. In order to produce the type of physical entertainment that fans demand requires bigger and faster players. That means that every time a player steps onto to field there is a very strong possibility of being severely injured.

For example, Patriots receiver Darryl Stingley spent the rest of his relatively short life in a wheelchair after a vicious hit from Jack Tatum. More recently, it was only by God's grace and some experimental medical technology that the life of Buffalo Bills' tight end Keven Everett was saved, after his neck was broken on kickoff coverage. So the price of seeing players perform at life threatening levels must be considered.

During the offseason, the Cleveland Browns offered me an opportunity to play for them and I was only hours from getting on that airplane to go to Cleveland, Ohio, just to talk to them.

Meanwhile, my wife Kim and I prayed very hard about where he wanted me to go. "Lord we want to be where you want us to be," we said.

At this point, the Panthers were not offering me the amount of money that I felt I was worth to the team. I knew that when I got to Cleveland they were going to make an offer to me that I could not refuse.

In spite of this, I still felt that the Lord wanted me to stay at Carolina. So I prayed again and said, "Lord, I know you said you want me to stay here, but the Panthers and I aren't on the same page." My agent had indicated to me that the Browns were going to offer me about four or five million dollars more than the Panthers. Regardless, I decided that I would take the Panthers offer if they would make the contract one million dollars more than they were offering, but the Panthers just wouldn't move.

We were at our pastor's house when the Cleveland coach, Butch Davis called me and said, "Okay Mike, are you ready? You got your plane tickets?"

I said to Coach Davis, "Yeah, I'm ready." My agent had already said to me that if I went to Cleveland, they would not let me leave until I had signed a contract with them.

I was still praying about what to do. I prayed, "Lord, it just doesn't look like it's going to happen. They don't seem willing to adjust their offer." I thought maybe God was telling me to go to Cleveland. After all it's where I was born and my dad's family was there. Maybe I was supposed to go back there and reconnect with them.

This decision reminded me so much of the night before I was to sign my letter of intent and I was asking the Lord, "Do I go to Nebraska or Baylor?" It was like I was at that same place in my mind that I was back in 1992. When I get to a place like this, I go to God for His direction.

"God, please give me some direction about this. What choice should I make?" I asked. This is one reason I know that God is real and He answers prayers. I can confirm that when you get in places where you don't know what to do, He will talk to you.

I finally said, "Lord, if you want me to stay here, I will, or I'll go to Cleveland. Wherever you want me to go, I'll go, but if I don't hear from Mr. Richardson by 12 midnight tonight, then I'm going to Cleveland.

I decided to talk to Mike Bunkley, the Carolina Panthers team chaplain. I said to him, "I really want to talk with Mr. Richardson."

I remembered that Mr. Richardson said something to me one day when Rocket Ishmael went to another team. Mr. Richardson and I were talking and he said, "Rocket never came to me and told me how he felt." That comment stuck with me. So I said, "I'm going to talk to him because sometimes you assume that the owner of the team knows what's going on and he doesn't. So I want to talk to him." I decided then that if I ever got in that position, I would go to Mr. Richardson and tell him what's going on.

That's when I asked Bunk, "Can you ask Mr. Richardson to call me?"

About five minutes later, the phone rang and it was Mr. Richardson. It was probably the deepest conversation we had ever had together. I said to him, "Mr. Richardson, I want to play for the Carolina Panthers. We're not very far off. I think we're a million dollars off. It's not a lot of money, but I have a chance to go to Cleveland and I know what they are going to offer me and its way more then what I'm asking to stay with the Panthers. I really want to stay here, though, because I love it here and I've always had a dream of only playing for one team in my NFL career."

I recalled that I had made that same statement to Eric Davis once. I had said to Eric, "I played for one team in college and I'm going to do the same thing in the NFL." Davis remembered that conversation and made a comment about that statement when the media interviewed him after I retired.

So Mr. Richardson said to me, "Okay."

We hung up the phone and about five minutes later the phone rang again. This time it was Coach Seifert. We hadn't talked at all but I knew he didn't want me to come back.

Coach Seifert said to me, "Mike, we really want you here and we want to make it work. We're going to get it done."

While he was talking to me I was thinking Coach Seifert, is it really you? What's going on?

At that moment God spoke to my spirit and said, "Mike there are things I want to do with you that are going to be good. Don't worry about it. It's going to be all good. I have plans to go to the Super Bowl." I liked that plan.

It just confirmed to me something I have always believed. The power of God makes people do things they don't want to do. It reminded me so much about the story of Moses when God got Pharaoh to tell the Israelites to leave. He didn't want to say it, but he said it anyway. This was definitely a situation that God worked to make it happen.

We hung up the phone and a about an hour later my agent called and said, "Mike they hit our number."

I said, "All right, let's get it done."

The most amazing thing about all of this is that all the negotiations were completed shortly before midnight Saturday night. Everything I had prayed about seemed to fall into place and I re-signed with the Carolina Panthers for five more years and $18 million, with $5 million up front.

I was supposed to fly out to Cleveland on Sunday morning but instead I went to my church. I was so happy that I was not going to have to move away from my church family. They had been praying for me about this situation, and I really did not want to leave my church because it was the first time that I had ever allowed people, outside of my family, to love me. During that ordeal, my church really became my church family.

That Sunday, Bobby, the youth pastor said to me in front of the congregation, "Mike, have you got something to say?" He had already talked to the pastor and knew what had happened with the team.

I'm not usually an emotional guy, but I got up and I said, "I thank you guys for being there and praying for me. I had a chance to go to Cleveland but we worked it out and I'm staying at Carolina." I was so emotional when I was talking that it took about ten minutes for me to say just a couple of sentences. My emotions just came out at that point, and everyone started clapping because I was going to stay here, in Charlotte.

After I signed my second contract, I bought my mama a house. I had wanted to buy it for her when I first signed with the NFL. I wanted her to move out of the neighborhood she lived in and into a nicer area. She had lived in Lawton View since she had returned from Cleveland. All of her friends were there, and also some of her family. She just wasn't ready to move. Most of her support system was either close by or in that neighborhood. After years of trying to convince her to move, she finally decided it was time after I re-signed with the Panthers in 2001.

I contacted a realtor in Lawton and told him to drive Mama around until she found the house she wanted. After several weeks, she chose a house and I told the realtor to make it happen. I wasn't able to be at the closing because I was at training camp, but I sent the money to complete the deal and my mama moved into her house. I tried to buy her new furniture, but she wouldn't hear of it. She wanted the old furniture that she had accumulated over the years. I guess it was her way of taking some of the old neighborhood with her.

One of the things my mama always did was to call me after every game and tell me that she had seen me. At first she couldn't get the games in Lawton, but she watched ESPN for the game highlights. Finally, I bought her Direct TV so she could actually watch every game. She was always so encouraging to me, and was also my biggest fan.

God had been telling me he wanted me to stay at Carolina and that He was going to do something good with me. I thought, great! We're going to win the Super Bowl. Little did I realize right then how much my faith would be tested during the coming season in 2001.

September 11, 2001 will always be a bittersweet day for Kim and I. During that past summer she had found out that she was pregnant. However, unlike her other pregnancies, this time she was carrying twins. Finally the day arrived for us to have the long awaited ultrasound. We arrived at the doctor's office, anxious to find out whether at least one of our new additions would be the girl we both desired, to complete our family of boys.

As Kim lay on the examination table and I sat on a chair beside her, we learned of the devastation that was occurring in New York City. At that moment we were focused on the new lives that would soon come into our world, but at the same time it was hard to take our eyes off of the news.

As the nurse slowly moved the wand across the wide expanse of Kim's abdomen looking for the signs of life within her, she looked at her screen and then looked at us.

"What are they?" We both asked with anticipation.

"I see one little girl, and yes, the other one is a little girl also."

We kissed and Kim began to cry. I'm sure she was happy about having girls, but I'm also convinced that she was thinking, how am I going to handle the two boys and two babies at one time? Nevertheless, we were both ecstatic that the babies were healthy as we left the office that day. It was sad though, that while we looked at the new life forming within Kim's body, others had lost theirs tragically and without reason.

My fifth season with the Carolina Panthers was unbelievable...and not in a good way. I don't think anyone could have predicted that the Panthers would fall so far. We won all the preseason games that year and the first game of the regular season against Minnesota 24-13. The team was so excited. Even Mr. Richardson was jumping around celebrating. Yes, we really thought the bad times were over and we were on our way to the Super Bowl. Everything was good. Then we went on to lose 15 games in a row. With each additional loss, George Seifert knew the writing was on the wall. He was going to get fired, and he began to distance himself from everyone.

I remember the last game we played was against the New England Patriots on January 6, 2002. We played that game at home in front of 71,907 fans and lost 38-6. We allowed five touchdowns and one field goal, while the Panthers were only able to muster two field goals for a total score of 6 points. It was a humiliating game that ended a season of lost hope and broken dreams. When I look back though, I think it is ironic to know now that the last team we played in the 2001 season would be the team we would face in the Super Bowl several years later. But one thing I can say unequivocally, no matter what the score or how many losses we had that season, Mike Minter never let up and never gave up. I was determined to play hard until the last whistle blew for this coach and well as any new coach who came to town.

All the good intentions and expectations did not mean a thing, because we lost every single game except one. The Carolina Panthers had once more made NFL history, but this time by losing more games in a row, in a single season, than any other NFL team. After the 2001 season, when we ended the season 1-15, I can remember thinking, what did I do? I cried out to God saying, did I hear you right? Maybe you did want me to go to Cleveland! I better check my life, because I thought I heard you say you wanted me here, but God, this is a disaster!

Needless to say, Dom Capers was right when he told us that when you're final record is 4-12, you get a new coach. That year we ended up 1-15, and just as with Capers, we got a new coach. At least Capers had walked away with the knowledge he had led the team to an NFC West championship. George Seifert walked away with the knowledge that the team he coached had the worst losing record in the NFL. He was fired the day after the season ended. To his credit though, he had put together a good team. Talent wasn't the issue here. Seifert just couldn't sell the dream.

As the team awaited the announcement of yet another new coach, I began to feel that I was never going to see the successes in professional football that I had experienced during my college years. To lose 15 games in a row is not fun, because the NFL is not fun unless you are winning.

Football is a sport of hard work, sweat, sacrifice and a whole lot of pain. Every Monday, every football player is in pain. The sheer violence of the collisions makes pain unavoidable. Getting out of bed can be an excruciating experience. Even tying your shoes can hurt. Winning makes the pain bearable. Losing just makes it worse. Also, losing can be just as contagious as winning and, once a team starts losing a lot, they begin to accept it more easily. This was a very dangerous place to be.

The sting of failures was only somewhat offset by the knowledge that I was now in a different place in my playing career. As a result of my new contract, I had moved from from a salary of $225,000 a year to over $2.5 million a year, with an upfront signing bonus of $5 million. I have to admit that it made the bitterness of all those defeats a little more bearable. Also, I began to feel the responsibility that God was putting on me to seek out ways in which I could help others. My philosophy is and has always been not to throw out money indiscriminately. Rather, my goal has become to help others reach a level in their lives by which they have the means and opportunity to help themselves.

That philosophy I carry with me into my family life as well. It is important to Kim and I that our children understand that the real world does not include people that give you things every time you turn around. In the NFL you have so many things that are given to you. It is hard for our children to separate their lives from reality. But, we want them to understand that in the real world doors don't always open the way you want and expect them to. We want them to be gracious for the opportunities that are given to them, and respectful of those people that give them. If I have learned anything in my life, I have learned that when you respect other people, they will respect you.

I use every moment possible to instill those values in my children. The way I parent is like a coach. Actually, it's the only way I know how. I try to look at things they have done wrong and instruct them. Sometimes I play out the best scenario for handling that situation if it presents itself again. I try my best to encourage them, but at the same time I can be strict.

I remember one time, however, that Michael had done something and I was so mad at him that I was ready to explode, and he was going to be the focus of my wrath. Then, God spoke to my heart and said, "You know Mike, that's how I feel sometimes when you have disappointed Me and gone against My will. How do you want Me to treat you in those circumstances?" Those thoughts suddenly brought me up short and I had to say, "Father, I would want you to give me another chance to prove myself to You."

"Very well then," God said in my heart. "Don't you think Michael might want that same chance?" I try to remember that conversation with God every time I'm put in a situation where I have to discipline my own children.

Chapter 8

JOHN FOX 2002-2003

He's a salesman selling a dream.

As January 2002 was ushered in, two events occurred that would change my life once again. John Fox was announced as the new coach for the Carolina Panthers on January 25, 2002, and on January 30, 2002, Kim gave birth to our twin girls, Brianna Nicole and McKenna Rose Minter.

The timing was perfect for their births because we were still in off season. It gave me the time to help Kim with our two new additions and I loved it. It brought back so many memories of when Michael and Isaiah were newborns and the hours I spent holding and feeding them. Those are joyous experiences that I will never forget, especially now, when I look at the tall, strapping teenager that Michael has become, followed closely by Isaiah. Our family was now complete, as I looked forward to the 2002 season. We had waited expectantly, once we learned Kim was carrying twins. The John Fox hiring however, was a complete surprise

The team had heard through the media that Steve Spurrier and Tony Dungy were both offered the job. John Fox was actually the third choice for the Panthers. We learned later that Spurrier and Dungy had turned it down. We knew Fox had been with the New York Giants as the defensive coordinator. Remember, the Giants had made it to the Super Bowl in 2000, along with having the first shutout in a conference game since 1986, so Fox wasn't a completely unknown candidate. But even knowing his credentials, we weren't sure what his effect would be on revitalizing the Panthers.

In the first team meeting Fox said to us, "Any team that loses 15 games in a row really doesn't have too much to say." Then he continued, "But I know what it means to be a champion and to create champions, and the guys that are in this room are going to become champions. I'm going to put this team together and basically I am looking for one type of player, someone who is smart and tough."

Smart and tough players were the ones that Fox surrounded himself with and, that's how the team was turned around. The guys that played for Fox in 2002 and 2003 understood the game and didn't make mistakes. They understood that when you get down to the fourth quarter with only two minutes left in the game and you have to make a play to win the game, you make the play. You don't buckle under pressure. They were tough.

Fox gave us direction and he gave us hope. He was hope. The same team that had gone 1-15 went to the Super Bowl two years later. That's due to leadership. Your leader has to dream and show you his dream and let you buy into it, in order for you to be successful. That's the way Coach Fox was back then. He was a leader who sold his dream. He let us buy in and let us know he was part of us. We were hungry for that. We were hungry for someone to come in and tell us that we were going to be winners and how we were going to get there.

When I met with him individually, Fox told me that he really liked how I played. He said, "You're going to be on my team and I look forward to working with you. We're going to let you run around and make some plays." I thought, man I like that!

Although George Seifert had built a good team, there was always something lacking. The team had talent, and that's what fans saw at the Super Bowl, but he just wasn't the leader that the Panthers needed. Then, Coach Fox came in and gave us that vision, and gave us a reason to win.

Fox's coaching staff came to our defensive group, which had been last in the NFL and told us that one reason we didn't win enough games is that we didn't finish plays and do the little things. Eventually, they taught us how to do those little things. Suddenly, the defensive team that had been last in the NFL under Seifert was second during that first year under Fox. What a difference a year can make, when the right people are at the helm. Even though the team involved the same key guys, our new leadership made such a difference. A team can have tremendous talent but without the leadership to put it together, you don't become winners. Under John Fox, the coaching staff believed in us and we made it happen.

Comparing the three coaches that I played under, I would have to say that they are all different. Fox is probably the most flexible. Like Capers, he is a defensive coach but Fox is a lot more flexible with the schedule. When Dom Capers was coach, whatever he had written on his chart was what we were going to do and how we were going to do it. But Fox, on the other hand, would change something if he felt it needed to be changed. While Capers was a no-nonsense type of coach, Fox would cut up with you, but he could also be no nonsense if he needed to be. Fox would sit down with you and talk. That's the way Fox is. He's a salesman and that's what you have to be to be a great coach. He would have a saying for everything and you just felt that he could take you to the top.

Jack DelRio, the defensive coordinator was the same way. He had passion and had played the game and understood how to win. He would say, "The defense looks like this on paper, but I know you can't do this because I played the game." If you missed a play he knew why you missed it and he didn't get mad. In the same situation, guys that hadn't played the game would get mad at you.

Fox and DelRio expected a lot, but I think if you expect a team to be champions then that's where they will go. I believe they expected us to be champions. They put their label on us and that's where we went.

I continue to believe that everything starts with the leadership. If the leader doesn't have passion and heart then the team won't have it. Players that don't want to play don't want to play because of the coach. It's not that guys don't want to win. When they step out on that field, everyone wants to win. When you have a team that is playing poorly, it isn't because they don't want to win. They're just tired of hearing the same old thing. That's when you need new leadership…leadership that inspires their players to play to the maximum of their abilities. In football you get to see the bad side of human nature, along with the good side, because it's played out on ESPN everyday. That's what football is all about.

The 2002 season was to be a rebuilding year for the Panthers. That year the Panthers drafted defensive end Julius Peppers, linebacker Will Witherspoon, and running back DeShaun Foster. It was clear that Fox was making adjustments to augment both our defensive and offensive teams, and, in retrospect, they were good moves.

Once more I entered the season enthusiastic that this would be our year to shine. Everything had settled down again with the new coaching staff and I was anxious for the new season to begin.

Then at practice one day, I received a panicked call from Kim.

"Mike, meet me at the hospital. Isaiah has cut off his finger."
I was on the phone trying to assimilate what Kim had just said, "What!" "What happened? What hospital?"

"Carolinas Medical at University, and hurry!" She said. "I'll fill you in when you get here."

I rushed to the hospital to find Kim and the doctors in a discussion about Isaiah's finger. He had been outside playing with some neighborhood children when a lawn chair he was trying to open, suddenly collapsed on his hand. However, in the rush to get him to the hospital, no one remembered to find the finger and bring it. The doctors told us that unless we could find that finger soon, there was a real possibility that Isaiah would have to go through the rest of his life with a missing digit on one hand.

One of the neighbors, who had brought Kim and Isaiah to the hospital, left immediately to look for the finger, while Kim and I remained there with Isaiah, praying for God's intervention. How they found the tiny end of his index finger I still do not know, but they did, and the first of many prayers were answered about that situation.

Once the finger had arrived at the hospital, though, another dilemma occurred. It had been severed for a while and had not been put on ice.

"There is no guarantee that the finger will seed properly, but we'll attach it and see what happens," the surgeon warned us.

Our immediate response was to return to God for one more request. I remembered the popular phrase often found on wall plaques, "It's me again Lord."

"Please let his finger heal properly," we asked the only One I knew who could intervene in this situation. "He is so small, and Lord, I just won't believe it is Your will for him to go through life without one of His fingers."

In his four short years, Isaiah had become our trooper. But, it was through his experiences and my own, that God was able to show me how much He cared for us. God had gotten me to the hospital before it was too late to save my leg or my life, and He had enabled the doctors to detect the cyst that threatened Isaiah's life. Now we were asking for life to come back into his finger. It was such a little thing for such a great God, I thought.

Each succeeding day Kim and I prayed and thanked God for the healing that we knew in our hearts was imminent. Then, about two weeks later, as the doctor surveyed the appendage, he smiled. "I think it's going to be okay," he said, and showed us the finger where a slight hint of new pink skin was growing. My spirit leapt so high that I could almost see the angels dancing in Heaven. Hallelujah! Kim and I looked at each other and without a doubt knew that God had once more brought our family through a very trying time. That's why I like to say to people, "don't give up on God, because He will never give up on you."

We began the 2002 season with three wins, but then followed those gains with eight losses in a row, losing twice to Atlanta, both at home and away. I think the question in everyone's mind was whether or not the Panthers were destined for a repeat of the previous year. But a funny thing happened on the way to yet another lost season. The leadership, hard work and determination of the coaching staff and team began to pay off. The coaches continued to encourage our efforts. They told us over and over that they believed in us and that we could come out of this slump. All we needed to do was continue to correct little things and we would come away with the victory. We won the next two games against

Cleveland and Cincinnati, but lost the following week to Pittsburgh. Finally, during the last two regular season games, it all seemed to come together. We beat Chicago 24-14 and then went on to play New Orleans in the last game of the season.

New Orleans had to win in order to go to the playoffs. It was a big game for them because everything was on the line. Nothing but a new-found pride was on the line for us. It was the first game that I had a taste of what a playoff game would feel like. It was a great game and we played it just as if we were in the playoffs. At the end of that game, which we won by a score of 10-6, I said, Man, we've got a team."

After we beat New Orleans in that last game, I began to see emerging, the championship team Fox envisioned. That year our defensive line went from a last place ranking in the NFL to second. We may have ended our season at 7-9, but it was a vast improvement over the 2001 season. It was the first time since my rookie year that I felt I could be a part of a championship team once more. It was exhilarating and I went to the 2003 training camp with the hopes and expectations I had left on a back burner after my rookie year with the Panthers.

When we began the 2003 season, I don't think any of us realized that we would be a Super Bowl team that year. Don't misunderstand me. Every team and every player has the Super Bowl as their goal when they begin their season. But the reality is that only two teams get invited. The Panthers had drafted Ricky Manning, Jr., a cornerback, and Jordan Gross, an offensive tackle. Quarterback Jake Delhomme, running backs Stephen Davis and Ricky Proehl had already been signed as free agents in the off season. With these additions, we felt very good about our offense...we already knew that we had a very solid defense.

In August, 2003, the Panthers again received more stunning news. Mark Fields, one of our very best offensive linebackers, was diagnosed with Hodgkin's disease, a cancer that attacks the lymph system. He would have to sit out the 2003 season while undergoing treatment. Not only was Fields an emotional leader on the team, but he was also a very significant player for a successful offense. During the previous season, Fields was recorded with 7.5 sacks as well as one interception. The tragedy of dealing with this disease was underscored by his loss to the team. Then, as if fate needed a slam dunk to discourage the team, Sam Mills, one of the most inspirational player/coaches to have been a part of the Panthers, announced that he had been diagnosed with intestinal cancer. Both men vowed to overcome their illnesses and a television campaign to bring attention to cancer research was initiated by the Carolina Panthers. "Keep Pounding" became a slogan for the Panthers and their fans.

In training camp that year, we started out competing hard. Normally, players tend to ease into the camp activities. Nobody, except some of the rookies, go full throttle when they first arrive at camp. But this particular year, we were pushing each other to make all the other players better. Sam Mills and Mark Fields became our inspiration and we were playing for them in addition to achieving our own dream of becoming a championship team. We came out showing our strength by winning all of our preseason games. Not only was our A-team the best, but our second and third teams were strong too.

Jake Delhomme, who had been with the New Orleans Saints, had signed on as the backup quarterback behind Rodney Peete, but won the starting position when Peete was replaced during the first game of the season. It was obvious when Peete began that opening game against Jacksonville that he was no match for the Jaguars defense or quarterback Mark Brunell. By halftime Peete had attempted only ten passes, completed four, been sacked three times and thrown for a total of 19 yards. On the other side of the field, Jacksonville had already scored 14 points. Seven of those points came from a 33-yard pass from Brunell to Matt Hatchett with only eight seconds left on the clock. In the third quarter, the Jaguars' Seth Marler, kicked a 40 yard field goal to make the Jaguar lead 17-0.

By the time Delhomme replaced Peete during the second half, the team had nothing to lose. Then, in the third quarter Delhomme hit Muhsin Muhammad with a 13 yard passed and he went in to score the Panthers first seven points of the game. The whole momentum of the game really changed for us in the fourth quarter when John Kasay kicked a 49 yard field goal. Jacksonville gave up a safety, which they incurred due to a bad snap deep in their own territory. The missed snap fell into the end zone where the kicker batted it out of bounds preventing the possibility of a touchdown by the Panthers. The error increased the Panthers score by 2 points, and with 12 minutes left in the game the Panthers were only six points away from the lead.

Six minutes remained in regulation when Delhomme fired a 24-yard pass to Steve Smith, putting us ahead 18-17. A two point conversion attempt failed. Then, Brunell went into action once more and fired a 65-yard pass to Jermaine Lewis who scored to put the Jaguars on top once more 23-18. The Jaguars also attempted a two point conversion which failed.

It was a heart stopping game, which led to the phrase "Cardiac Cats" and it stuck. With only 22 seconds left in the game Delhomme threw a 12-yard pass to Ricky Proehl who scored to put us ahead 24-23. The final play of the game came after Mark Brunell threw a pass to Matt Hatchette. He was run out of bounds at the Carolina 37-yard line, but it still put them in position for a field goal. As we lined up, Seth Marler was set to kick a 55-yard field goal, but at the last second, I broke through the blocking and got my hand on the ball, deflecting their attempt.

The game ended in an amazing turnaround for the Panthers. I was so excited that I threw my helmet off and ran and jumped in the stands with the fans. I guess you might call it the down home version of the "Lambeau Leap." I was probably the most excited I've ever been after a football game. It is interesting to note that when fans and sports writers remember that game they always talk about the touchdown by Rickie Proehl. They seem to forget the fact that Jacksonville could have won that game had we not been able to block that last field goal attempt. That's what the defense is paid to do and that time we did it. It just goes back to the little things in the last minutes of play that can make the difference between a winner and loser.

It was a great game for the Panthers and an even greater feeling for me because I could see our defense was really solid. If our offense could just hold the line now, we could be the champions that John Fox had promised we would become. The way we beat Jacksonville that year was magical and you've got to have some magic in a great season.

We won the first five games of the 2003 season, which included a 23-20 win against Indianapolis, in overtime. It was also the first time we had beaten Atlanta, our arch rival, at home, since the 1999 season, and we did it in a 23 -3 victory. We weren't just winning we were physically pounding those other teams.

When you have something special, everybody feels it. Everybody feels the energy. It's an amazing thing. Enthusiasm and energy are the difference between a dead team and one that is alive. The team that is dead has no spirit or energy or life. That's the difference I felt between my first year as a rookie and the Panther team of 2003. Halfway through the season we had won eight out of ten games. Then, the magic left as quickly as it had arrived, and we racked up three losses in a row-all to big contenders, Dallas, Philadelphia and Atlanta. Fortunately it returned, and the following three games were all wins. With each win we accumulated during the last three games of the regular season, we knew for sure that we were on our way to the head of the line.

The Panthers were 11-5 when our regular season ended and had secured the NFC South Conference far ahead of New Orleans who went 8-8 that year. Tampa Bay and Atlanta both recorded losing seasons. We were headed for a playoff berth and we were ready.

The playoffs began Saturday, January 3, 2004 with the wildcard games. The Tennessee Titans were pitted against the Baltimore Ravens and we would be taking on the Dallas Cowboys.

During the first drive of the first quarter, our offense definitely set the tone of that game as Jake Delhomme completed a 70-yard pass to Steve Smith in a third down situation. The ball was placed on the one yard line which set up the first field goal of the game for John Kasay. Later, with three points already on the board, the Panthers received a punt from Dallas on the Cowboys 41-yard line and that great field position allowed us to move the ball downfield to score yet another field goal. Dallas tried to answer when they got a first down at the Carolina 20-yard line. As the Cowboys tried to make something out of their red-zone offense, Richie Anderson fumbled the ball and I recovered it for Carolina putting an end to the Dallas drive for points in the first quarter.

Late into the second quarter, Stephen Davis ran the ball 23-yards into the end zone with a good point after, to give us a 13-0 lead. Dallas kicked a field goal that quarter, putting them on the board 13-3. After the subsequent kickoff, Delhomme completed a 57-yard pass to Muhsin Muhammad which set up the third field goal for Carolina in the game. The half ended with the score Carolina 16, Dallas 3.

In the third quarter, Steve Smith received a punt from Dallas and ran it seven yards to the Panthers' 37-yard line. Muhammad continued the drive when he caught a 24-yard pass, followed by a 7-yard pass and capped the drive with a 32-yard touchdown pass. The score was now 23-3 and Dallas was reeling from the domination that the Panthers had shown in this game. Before the third quarter had ended, Muhammad returned a punt from Dallas to the Carolina 40-yard line. Subsequently, a 38-yard drive ended with a fourth field goal by John Kasay, increasing our lead 26-3.

Dallas tried hard to rally its position, which was weakening by the minute. Quincy Carter completed six consecutive passes that would lead to a nine yard touchdown run late in the fourth quarter. But the final blow came from our defense when Julius Peppers intercepted a screen pass and returned it to the Cowboys 11-yard line setting up the fifth field goal of the game for Carolina. With only three minutes left in the game, the Panthers had secured a 29-10 victory, and were now ready to move on to the divisional playoffs.

The divisional playoffs were held on January 10, 2004 and 29 must have been our lucky number that year. The first quarter played out with no score by either team. The Panthers tried to get in sync as the Saint Louis Rams defense were able to hold on and prevented us from encroaching into Rams territory. With three minutes into the first quarter the Rams put together a drive that lasted more then seven minutes and resulted in a field goal. Carolina got the ball to the St. Louis 43-yard line but was stopped when Delhomme's pass to Steven Davis was intercepted. The first quarter ended with St. Louis on top 3-0.

During the second quarter we began to gain speed again when Muhammad scored a touchdown. Even though St. Louis challenged the play, the ruling was upheld and Kasay went on to kick the extra point. St. Louis attempted to answer and got the ball to the Carolina 6-yard line but stalled there and was forced to settle once more for a field goal. Carolina put together a drive that would take us to the 27 yard line. Kasay kicked again and added another three points to our score.

At the half the score was Carolina 10, St. Louis 3 and we were on a roll, we thought. At the beginning of the third quarter St. Louis was set to receive the ball and drove it to the Carolina 33-yard line where St. Louis quarterback, Marc Bulger, threw an incomplete pass setting up a 51-yard field goal attempt for Jeff Wilkins. St. Louis scored and we answered with a 52-yard field goal kick by John Kasay. The Rams got the ball back with no results. With seven minutes left in the third quarter, we put together a drive that would take the clock to the 50 second mark. Kasay kicked another field goal from 37-yards out to make the score 16-9, Carolina.

Through three quarters of this game our defense held the Rams to a total of three field goals. It was now down to the final quarter of the game and the Rams once more got the ball with no results. Then with less then nine minutes left in the game Brad Hoover ran seven yards for a touchdown and Kasay kicked the extra point.

If we thought we were secure with a 23-9 lead and only 8 minutes left in the game we should have reflected back to the 2001 season when we ended 1-15. That year twelve of those 15 games were lost in the last two minutes of the game, after Carolina has secured large leads. The remaining three games were lost with less then three minutes left on the clock.

With six minutes left in the game, the Rams drove the ball to the Carolina three yard line where a penalty was assessed on Carolina that moved the ball to the one yard line. On the third down the Rams pushed into the end zone and then completed a two point conversion attempt to make the score now 23-20, Carolina. Then St. Louis kicked onside which they recovered and with three seconds left on the clock Jeff Wilkins kicked the tying field goal, making the score 23-23 as the clock ran out.

If you can see your past flash before your eyes, our team saw it then. We had come back from the worst losing season in NFL history, with the worst defense, to win a wildcard slot. As we went into overtime, we wondered if we had it in us to make that play, when the pressure is on, that would win the game.

Somehow, we just knew this would be different. We wanted it to be different for the coaching staff that had supported us, for Sam Mills and Mark Fields who inspired us, and for ourselves, because we wanted this game more than any we could remember.

On the first overtime drive we charged down the field to the Rams 22-yard line where Kasay easily made the 40-yard field goal attempt. In an ironic twist of fate though we were flagged for a Delay of Game which moved the ball back five yards. Kasay's second attempt went wide right and the ball was turned over to the Rams on their 45-yard line. St. Louis proceeded to move the ball into Carolina territory where Jeff Wilkins attempted a 53-yard field gold. It too fell short. The scoreless period coupled with a Ricky Manning, Jr. interception, as St. Louis drove the ball into Carolina territory, sent the game into a second overtime.

It was time to act and on the first drive of the second overtime, Jake Delhomme hailed a 69-yard touchdown pass to Steve Smith to win the NFC divisional playoff game. The playing time on the field was 75:10. In had been the longest game in NFL history since 1987 when the Cleveland Browns beat the New York Jets 23-20 in the AFC divisional playoff. That game lasted 77:02. The longest game in NFL history was the AFC divisional playoff on December 25, 1971 between the Miami Dolphins and the Kansas City Chiefs. That game lasted 82:40 before Miami ended it with a 27-24 victory.

On January 18, 2004 the Carolina Panthers faced our arch nemesis, the Philadelphia Eagles, in the NFC Championship, and the game was played at Philadelphia. It was a bitter cold 33° when we took the field at Lincoln Financial Field that night. Our anticipation was at its zenith. We knew that the key to winning this game would be to limit Donovan McNabb's ability to make the big plays. We knew the game would probably be a low scoring game. Their defense was sure to be brutal to our Panthers offense. Our defensive team playing at its all-time best would be crucial to our winning the game. We tasted victory and we were not going to allow the Eagles to take it away from us now.

We began first quarter with the prime objective of shutting down their offense, which we did. That quarter we held the Eagles to only one field goal. We just kept pounding and not letting up. The first sack of the game came with just two and a half minutes left in the first quarter. Will Witherspoon managed to sack McNabb for a 7-yard loss. The quarter ended with no score.

The second quarter opened with Carolina still in control of the ball. Our offense was able to put together a drive that lasted over five minutes but resulted in a touchdown, putting Carolina ahead 7-0.

The Eagles responded with a six minute drive in which McNabb was sacked by Mike Rucker with just 4 minutes and 22 seconds left in the half. The sack resulted in a rib injury but McNabb refused to leave the game. He managed to get the ball to the Carolina 23-yard line where David Akers kicked a 41-yard field goal to end the half 7-3. McNabb was sacked two additional times that quarter, once by myself and Brentson Buckner, and at the end of second quarter by Buckner again, with only 15 seconds remaining on the clock. The constant pounding was taking a toll on McNabb.

As we returned to the locker room for halftime, we knew we had this game if we could just keep getting to McNabb. We could see the results already with the number of incomplete passes and the four sacks that we had already racked up against McNabb. Our defensive line was on a roll and we knew it. The Philadelphia time of possession had been almost four more minutes more than the Panthers. It was our defense that kept them from converting that time to scoring points.

The second half began with the Eagles receiving the ball. McNabb took longer then usual coming out of the tunnel. We knew he must be hurt, but he continued to play. He managed to get off five passes during the third quarter. Only one of them was completed, two were incomplete and two were intercepted. During the last interception, tight end James Thrash of the Eagles was the intended receiver. Ricky Manning, Jr. caught the interception and I got the tackle on Thrash at the 50-yard line. After the play ended Philadelphia called a timeout because Thrash had been shaken up on that play. Our defense was working like a clock. When play resumed, the Eagles received a defensive pass interference call, which moved the ball to the Philadelphia 15-yard line with four minutes left in the quarter. Our offense was able to take the ball into the end zone with a one yard touchdown run by Deshaun Foster. The extra point was good and the third quarter ended with Carolina on top 14-3.

As the fourth quarter began there was a tense moment when Steve Smith fumbled the ball on the Carolina 45-yard line. Philadelphia recovered, but the play was challenged and reversed, allowing the Panthers to maintain the ball. Our defense was phenomenal against an offense that continued to move the ball in spite of injury to the quarterback. A severely hurt McNabb was replaced by quarterback Koy Detmer, who was able to move the ball 74 yards to the Panthers 11-yard line. However, with only five minutes left in the game, Dan Morgan intercepted the ball and we took possession once more. Then with just two minutes 23 seconds left in the game, Shane Burton and I were able to sack Detmer with a loss of seven yards on the 50-yard line. Two more incomplete passes by Detmer allowed Carolina to take a knee and put one more championship game under our belts.

Now we were ready for the big one. Looking back it was such a magical year for the Panthers! What created that magic? I believe it was a combination of things. I believe it was the sudden awareness that we could be champions, if we just believed in ourselves and the dream was sold to us by John Fox and reinforced by his coaching staff. I think it was the constant inspiration that Sam Mills and Mark Fields provided to us that year. I certainly think that George Seifert has to be commended for putting together most of the talent in that 2003 team. Finally, it was the dedication of the Carolina fans that watched us with dismay during the 1-15 season but returned to cheer us on as we made our way to victory that momentous year.

I will always remember fondly our old neighborhood, in Charlotte. Many times when I returned from a game, I was greeted by signs at all the houses in our neighbors' yards which read "Good game Mike," whether or not we won on lost that year. The day I left for the Super Bowl, it was icy and cold, yet our neighbors stood outside as I left and waved at me and wished the team luck in the upcoming game.

Chapter 9

SUPER BOWL XXXVIII AND BEYOND

⁷"Some trust in chariots and some in horses, but we trust in the name of the LORD our God. ⁸ They are brought to their knees and fall, but we rise up and stand firm." Psalms 20:7-8 (NIV)

February fourth two thousand four-a day I will never forget. For a city whose typical weather averages around 67º F Houston, Texas was a welcome change from the bitter cold we experienced previously in Philadelphia.

The team had flown to Houston the week before the game. Our families followed but the NFL made arrangements for them to stay at a different hotel for obvious reasons. I secured the rental of a limo service which would drive my family and me wherever we wanted to go that week. Kim, our children, Michael, Isaiah, Brianna and McKenna, Dan and Debbie Rose, their son Austin, who is the same age as our son Michael, my mama, sister Boo and her friend and my brother Chewy all traveled to Houston that week to see the game. As exciting as it was for me, I believe it was even more exciting for them. During the week leading up to the big game we had a wonderful time. The people of Houston welcomed and encouraged us wherever we went.

Game time was five o'clock. Carolina won the toss and the New England Patriots kicked off. It was not the start we had hoped for, but there was still a lot of game left to play. After three consecutive downs we had to punt to the Patriots. New England put together a drive that moved the ball downfield where Will

Witherspoon and I were able to stop Atowain Smith at the Carolina 18. After a penalty against Carolina moved the ball to the 13-yard line, Adam Vinatieri missed a 31-yard field goal when it sailed wide right. The quarter ended with no score for either team.

Our defense seemed to be holding the Patriots as the clock ticked down to the six minute mark when the Patriots again moved the ball into field goal range. This time the kick was blocked by Shane Burton and the ball rolled into the end zone. At this point the Patriots and the Panthers were head to head, each team striving to put the first points on the board. Then, with just five minutes left in the half, Jake Delhomme was sacked on the Carolina 19-yard line for a loss of six yards and then fumbled the ball. The Patriots then put together a drive that moved the ball all the way to the Carolina five yard line where I made the tackle. Patriots quarterback, Tom Brady, put it into the end zone and Vinatieri redeemed his earlier miss with the extra point. The score was 7-0, New England. With three minutes left in the half, we answered with a drive that also resulted in a touchdown and a good extra point, making the score 7-7. The Patriots answered with another touchdown, with only 23 seconds left in the half. With the extra point, New England made the score 14-7. Carolina received the ball and got it to the New England 32-yard line where John Kasay completed a 50-yard field goal with no time left on the clock. At halftime the score stood at 14-10. It was a tough defensive game, but we were holding our own.

Halftime that year will always be remembered by Janet Jackson's poorly chosen antics at the end of a dynamic musical performance. Although she may go into the hall of NFL memories as the most talked about show, the negative response she received from the NFL barred her performing at an NFL championship game again.

The team was encouraged as we began the third quarter that evening in Reliant Stadium. As the clock wound down to just under six minutes, Carolina received the ball on their own 18-yard line but was assessed a 10-yard penalty that moved the ball back to the eight. The subsequent drive never got the ball past the 14-yard line and Todd Sauerbrun's 47-yard punt gave the Patriots excellent field position on their 39-yard line. A drive that lasted just short of four minutes put the Patriots in scoring position on the Carolina four yard line to end the quarter.

The fourth quarter is one that will be remembered for many years among NFL fans. It began with a penalty on Carolina which moved the moved the Patriots ball to the Carolina two yard line. With less than a minute into the fourth quarter, Antowain Smith made it into the end zone for another New England touchdown. The Panthers were not going to be outdone and answered with a drive that lasted only two minutes and 18 seconds, resulting in a touchdown. With 12 minutes left in the game the score was now New England 21, Carolina 16.

New England was gaining momentum as Tom Brady rapidly moved the ball down into scoring position again, but in a turn of events the pass, which would have added another 6 points to New England's score, was intercepted in the end zone by Carolina Panther, Reggie Howard. We turned the gift into another touchdown but failed in the two point conversion attempt putting Carolina ahead for the first time at 22-21.

The clock was at six minutes and the Patriots answered again with another touchdown in another four minute drive downfield. Their two-point conversion succeeded and the Patriots jumped in front again 29-22.

At this point, neither defense held, and it became a bitter battle to determine which offensive team could hold out the longest. We were determined not to be out-done, and marched down the field in a one-minute, forty-three second drive for another touchdown which tied the score at 29-29. There was only a minute left in the game and sports announcers were already saying that this would be the first overtime played in Super Bowl history.

The last minute of that game I'm sure I will play out in my mind for a long, long time. Our unfortunate loss began when John Kasay kicked the ball out of bounds at the New England 18-yard line, which resulted in the Patriots getting it on their 40-yard line. Then a series of shotgun plays by the Patriots moved the ball into field goal range at the Carolina 23. As the clock ticked down to nine seconds, Adam Vinatieri did not let his team down on this kick. The ball sailed through the goal posts to make the score New England 32, Carolina 29. My heart sank.

If there was one play in my whole football career that I wish I could replay, it would be the one just before New England scored the winning field goal. I saw the guy break, but I was trying to be cautious. I was so sure that I could knock the ball out and that's what I was trying to do. I hit that guy harder than I've ever hit anybody. I must have knocked him back at least five yards, but he still held onto the ball. If I could have just knocked that ball out, we would have gone into overtime and maybe had a chance to win.

Once the game had ended, the losing team is hurried off the field in order to make the preparations for the winner's trophy awards. My mind traveled back in time and I remembered my first year of football when we lost the championship to Douglas Elementary. I learned then there was no second place in a championship game and it was reconfirmed to me now as I ran into the locker room. There is only the winner and the loser.

During each of the play-off games, I had written a Scripture verse on my gloves and given them to Jerry Richardson, saying to him that we were going to give him the championship game. This time I said, "Mr. Richardson, I am sorry. I apologize that this is one pair of gloves that I can't give you because we didn't deliver to you what we had promised."

I have to admit, it was very hard to lose this game. A winners' party had been organized for after the game, which was held in spite of the loss, but I couldn't bring myself to attend. In fact, I didn't even want to be with my family that night. I just wanted to be alone.

In retrospect, to have the opportunity to play in the Super Bowl was a dream that came true for me. In my entire football career, the only two things I was not able to accomplish was winning the Super Bowl and being named as a Pro Bowler, although, I was chosen as an alternate twice. Looking back, I'm happy that I was able to accomplish as much as I have in a game that I love so much.

We left the elation of the 2003 season and the 2004 Super Bowl behind and focused our attentions on returning to the Super Bowl the following year.

Three things define the 2004 year. First, we were 1-7 during the first half of the season. We lost games that were unbelievable. We would pull ahead by a huge margin until the last quarter of the game. Then, in game after game, we gave up the win.

Halfway through the season, we were scheduled to play San Francisco. I finally pulled the team together for a team meeting and said to them, "Guys, look. I know what it's like to be 1 and 15 and we don't want to go there. We need to get our act together. We need to begin to play with some pride and finish this season up. You don't want to end up 1-15. The coaches get fired. You get fired and that's not where we want to go. We need to step up. Go down to San Francisco and beat these boys and get on track for the rest of the season."

Then Moose spoke up and confirmed what I said, because he was also on that 1-15 team. I wasn't sure whether what we said impacted the team or not, because sometimes it works and sometimes it doesn't.

We went to San Francisco and bombed during the first half. We weren't playing well at all. Then in the second half, all of a sudden Moose went crazy catching all kinds of balls. We reacted on defense by making turnovers. All of a sudden, the game just turned around and with it, our whole season.

I really believe it began when Mark Fields intercepted the ball and ran it down almost for a touchdown. That sparked the team and I believed it changed our whole season. We went on to win six out the last eight games. I saw the heart of our team at that time, and it was the heart of a lion. We weren't going to lie down. I saw that Coach Fox had the ability to get people to step out of the situation and play beyond it. He had what it took as a coach to do it. I knew then that this team was different than the one that played the 1-15 season. We didn't have quitters on this team. We had people who cared and had pride. At that moment I knew that the team was going to be fine.

The second defining event of the 2004 season was personal. At that time I was selected as a Pro Bowl alternate, so it was a time in my life that I began to receive recognition for my playing. I was recognized as Pro status. It was important to me. After seven years in the NFL, I had made a mark.

The third defining event that year was the fact that my second contract was coming to an end that season and I was now into negotiations for my third and final contract. This one would make me a Panther for life. The contract negotiation was totally different this time. I wanted to end my career as a Carolina Panther and Coach Fox and Mr. Richardson wanted me to stay with the Panthers also. I knew that we would come up with a deal that both parties would be happy about. I told my agent, just get the deal done. It wasn't about the money this time. The Panthers and my agent, Craig Doman, communicated well. From the Panthers viewpoint, I was at the end of my career so they didn't want to give me a pay raise but they still wanted me to stay with the team. I wanted to be there. I told Craig if they would continue to pay me what I had been making I would be happy. We inked that deal at $14 million with a $5 million signing bonus before my second contract ended. It was the most comfortable that I had felt since I came into the NFL. I believe that the last contract was a thank you for all the things I had done for the team over the years. I felt it was a tribute for the respect I had for the ownership of the team, and for the respect they had for me. Of course, I had to perform on the field and do what I was supposed to do, but that contract was really about respect for doing it right over the years.

That's the most important thing I try to say to people. Do it right and you'll be rewarded for it. You may not get rewarded right up front but you'll be rewarded. It's never smart to burn bridges or do it your way, or be all about yourself. If you just do the right thing, at the end of the day, you'll get it back.

That year we seemed to finally get it all together. The only thing that kept us from that coveted playoff berth was our nemesis, Atlanta. We played the Falcons at home, in a Saturday night game, December 18, 2004. It was the fourth with less than two minutes left in the game. The score was Carolina 31-24. The Falcons had gotten the ball to our two yard line, but were backed up due to a penalty. With only a minute and 30 seconds left in the game, they were fourth and 12. All we had to do was to hold them on this one down, and the game and playoff berth were ours. Then, Vick did one of his famous scrambles to run the ball into the end-zone. When he reached the five yard line, he just dove, literally floating off the ground, into the end zone to tie the game. The play was even reviewed by the officials to see if his knee had touched the ground, but the call was upheld. Somehow he had been able to keep it up. The touchdown sent the game into overtime, which resulted in a field goal by the Falcons, ending the game 34-31. It was a discouraging loss after we had fought so hard to come back.

We came into the 2005 season enthusiastic. Steve Smith was healthy and back on the team, after sustaining a broken leg injury at the beginning of the last season. However, we lost Moose to the Chicago Bears. It was tough for the team, and for me, personally.

That year was the first time that the Panthers were able to beat the Atlanta Falcons at home, with Michael Vick as quarterback. I attribute this in part to a new defense strategy where Thomas Davis was assigned the job of chasing Vick, in order to contain him and not allow him outside the pocket. We were able to succeed at the task, which took our game to the next level.

I think the biggest moment for us as a team that year was when we won the wildcard. A big detriment though, was the fact that our last two games that season, and the playoff games, were all on the road. There was also a tremendous difference between this playoff season and 2003, when we went to the Super Bowl. We had already clinched the playoff berth before the 2003 season ended. So we had some games we could lay back in, put in the second team and allow the first team to rest. In 2005 we couldn't do that because we lost so many games at the beginning of the season. We had to win all the last games then play the New York Giants in a wildcard game. Eli Manning was quarterback and the Giants thought they were going to pass the ball all over us, but we had a great game and shut them out 23-0. I felt at that time we were going to win it all.

Chicago was the determining game for us because we had played them in the regular season and they beat us. We were confident that if we beat Chicago in the divisional round of the playoffs, we would go all the way to the top this time. We were victorious in Chicago and won 29-21, but by then we were a tired football team. I really believe that we wanted to win against Chicago so badly that we put everything we had into that game. Afterwards, we were both physically and emotionally drained.

The road to the NFC Championship game was intense for us that year. We had to play five games back to back games on the road. The Seattle game was on the west coast. By that time, we were far from peak in our performance. Plus, Seattle is the loudest stadium I have ever played in. The weather was terrible. It poured down rain. Everything about that game was miserable. Seattle was sharp and fast. Everything we did was one step behind and we could never get into a rhythm. But I believe we lost that game because we were a simply a tired football team.

Seattle was a well prepared team. They did a good job taking Steve Smith out of the game. We really didn't have a running game because all our running backs were hurt. We went in there fighting a strong opponent with one hand tied behind our backs.

During the game the defense was on the field a lot. One play I remember was a busted coverage and Seattle's tight end caught the ball and ran it in for a touchdown. I believe that was the play that broke the game open for Seattle. The whole time though, the Panther team was never in sync. It was never a situation where we were in control. We were always on our heels. They were getting out of that huddle so fast that we couldn't get into a rhythm to react. I think the significance of the game was the speed of it and the way they were coming at us. We didn't have time to breathe. They just had a great game and we had a poor one.

By the end of the 2005 season, I was really tired and my mind was fatigued. After the season was over I was not sure if I could go through the rigor too much longer. I started thinking about how grueling the whole season had been. I knew I couldn't continue to put the same effort I had in the past-the kind that it takes in order to make it to the Super Bowl. To get to the Super Bowl, you've got to pay a price. You've got to put it all on the line-everything, mentally, physically-the whole nine yards. I began to realize that I didn't have too much left to lie down. So I started thinking at that point that my career was definitely coming to an end. Then, in the off-season, I was running, but I wasn't really running the way I needed to, in order to get in shape. My breathing wasn't right and I had to work hard to try to get in shape and that was the first time that I felt old. This was different for me. It was a struggle to do the things I needed to do to get in shape.

During the summer of 2006, I anticipated that the next year was going to going to be a tough road for me. I was getting tired and really ready to move into the next phase of my life, but I thought that the team had a chance to do something special. My knees weren't giving me trouble at that point.

Then I received the word that Mama was in the hospital and not expected to survive. It was a summer that I will remember for the rest of my life. After her funeral, I was in a different state and the 2006 season proved to be my toughest yet, for a lot of reasons.

The first preseason game of 2006 was coming up that next week against Washington but I didn't play. I watched it on television to see how we were doing. After the funeral and going through all the emotional things regarding Mama's death, I went into a state of shock and depression. It was tough to deal with the fact that Mama was gone and she wasn't going to be there anymore. She had been one of the most important people in my life. I loved her so much and now she wouldn't be around to encourage me. Returning to the team and trying to get back into football, just wasn't the same.

The year of 2006 became a floating year for me. It was grueling, both mentally and physically, and the first year that playing football was no longer fun for me. It was the worst time in my life, not one game was fun. I knew as I was going through that year that I was worn out physically. Then the emotional situation just drained me. I tried my best to muster the excitement, energy and enthusiasm necessary to play football effectively, but it just wasn't there anymore. I remember the first game that I played that season, as the National Anthem played I was crying. I was devastated as I thought about Mama and the fact that she wasn't watching me.

When we kicked the ball off to them, I ran onto the field crying. I went into the huddle thinking about my mama. It took me four or five games to get back into the mix. That year I might have had one or two games where I felt that I was playing good football. The rest of the year, I didn't play well. I knew then that 2006 was probably going to be my last season, but I wanted to take some time to heal. I wanted to take some time to think about whether it was even feasible for me to begin the 2007 season.

Coach Fox and Marty Hurney and I sat down and talked. I told them, I really wanted to finish my career on the field. They understood, but at the same time they told me they weren't guaranteeing I would start the 2007 season. I said that was fine with me. It wasn't the first time that I had to beat out the competition.

During the off season I didn't train that hard because I wanted to give my knees time to heal. I spent most of my time just talking to God. I knew this was the end of the road in my football career. I spent time trying to understand what the league is all about. It's a strange feeling to know that you're about to give up something that you had been doing your entire life. Some days I felt okay and some days the world just wasn't right. I fought through all that and got to training camp. I had to say to myself that I knew what it took to get through camp. I felt that I would know within a week if I was going to be able to complete another season. Before I even made my decision I talked with the team and told them it was time for me to go. Then I talked with Mr. Richardson. He said, "We all knew that this time would come one day." I apologized to him that I was never able to give him that last glove, which meant we had won a Super Bowl for him.

My two biggest disappointments, over my nine year career in the NFL, were that although I was chosen as a Pro Bowl alternate, I never actually played in the Pro Bowl game. And, that the Carolina Panthers were not able to win the Super Bowl.

When the reports of the New England Patriots spying attempts were revealed during the 2007 season, the question was asked with regard to that Super Bowl Sunday. Did that advantage equate to the three point difference between the winner and the loser of that game? The answer will never be known for sure. I will say that it had to have helped them. If you know what the plays your opponent is going to make, you can more easily decide how you will respond. However, you still have to execute and make the plays and they did that well. I just hope that if we meet the Patriots in the Super Bowl once more, we will be able at that time to exact retribution.

Chapter 10

REMEMBERING MAMA

"Many women do noble things, but you surpass them all."
Prov 31:29 (NIV)

There is nothing in football or in life that can prepare you for the loss of someone you love dearly. Even my most challenging moments, both on and off the field, never took me to the depths of emotion that I felt when Mama died. She had been the person who supported and encouraged me throughout all my endeavors as I was growing up. She was the one who told me that I would do something very special one day. I had believed her dream and achieved the success she had predicted. Yet, there was so much more that I wanted to do for her. I can say from this experience that there will never be enough time to show someone how much you love them. All you have is now, and all you can do is make the most of today. Even though she knew I cared about her, in my mind the expression of my thankfulness was never completely fulfilled. I thought there was more time. I never anticipated that at 59, Mama would be gone so soon.

In spite of the unquenchable sadness that permeated my mama's funeral, it was still a celebration that she would have been thrilled to attend. Still, I cried more that day then I have ever cried in my entire life. As each memory of all the things she had done for me darted through my mind, I would cry a little harder.

By the time we arrived at the church, I couldn't raise my head up. I wore my sunglasses so no one could see my face and know how much I had been crying. The ushers carefully led us to a pew, at the front of the church, where the warm-gray colored casket sat surrounded by perfumed flowers. The spray which had been carefully placed on top of the coffin was filled with orchids and roses-her favorites.

The church was filled to overflowing. Mama would have been ecstatic to see so many people at her funeral. There were the store clerks who had waited on her-all the way up to the city officials. Plus, of course, Jerry and Mark Richardson, Marty Hurney, John Fox as well as Mike Rucker, who all came to the funeral. They represented the notable contingent from my team, the Carolina Panthers. It was an expression of sympathy that I will never forget. To me it was another example of the type of leadership that makes up the Carolina Panthers, from the owner, Mr. Richardson to the general manager, Marty Hurney and Head Coach, John Fox. Even my close friend, Mike Rucker, left training camp to come to the funeral.

In fact, so many people wanted to attend the service that we had to move it from Calvary Baptist to Bethlehem Baptist Church. What a compliment to the woman whose fantasy of being a movie star never ceased to make us laugh. She had told us that dream time after time as we were growing up. This was her final stage, her swan song appearance and she would have loved the attention.

I thought about one of Mama's predictions. She had declared many times that when she died, there would be so many people at her funeral that we would need a bigger church. She said it, not because she thought that she would ever be famous, but because she always anticipated my success. I believe it was also one of her dreams, and today she had become a celebrity of sorts, a queen for a day.

The minister opened the service by quoting from Psalm 46 from the Bible.
"God is our refuge and strength, an ever-present help in trouble."
Psalms 46:1 (NIV)

The words hardly registered to me during the service, even though I had found over the past ten years the truth of that statement. Then, he proceeded to quote from the Book of Isaiah.

"He gives strength to the weary and increases the power of the weak. Even youths grow tired and weary, and young men stumble and fall; but those who hope in the LORD will renew their strength. They will soar on wings like eagles; they will run and not grow weary, they will walk and not be faint."
Isaiah 40:29-31 (NIV)

Yes, I thought. Mama, I can see you now, soaring like an eagle in flight, looking down at your family from your heavenly throne. There is no more pain or tears, and the happiness of being there with your Heavenly Father must be more than we who are still alive, can even begin to comprehend.

Yet, regardless of the joy I felt for Mama, at that moment the pain I was experiencing was deeper than any ocean. The knowledge that even though Mama was safe from all the hurt in her life did not console me. I knew I would see her eventually, but it would not be while I was still on earth. That thought cut deeply into the core of my spirit.

During the arrangements for the service and burial, the funeral home personnel had asked if the family wanted an opportunity to view the body one more time after the service was over. Most of the family said yes, but I could not bring myself to look at Mama lying so still in her final bed. That would have been too much like saying goodbye, and I was still not entirely ready to do that. I realize that makes no logical sense, but at times like this, logic is a big time loser to the emotion of it all.

The service had concluded and the entire church was cleared, except for the family. Each person went to her casket one more time to say goodbye. Everyone that is, except for me. I was still sitting with my head down. My face was covered by a towel that one of the ushers had handed me early and I could not bring myself to lower it, even for a moment. As I held it tightly in place against my face, I searched for an answer, any answer…yet I didn't really have a question…it was just my way of escaping the moment.

The ushers began to move the casket into the isle, but it was still not closed.

As they maneuvered it, I raised my head for only a second and found the casket setting directly in front of me. At that instant I looked at Mama, and felt as though electricity was shooting through my whole body. Suddenly I lost all my control. To say I was devastated would not fully convey what I was feeling. I guess when I saw her, it really hit me that she was gone. I cried even more freely into the towel already drenched from my tears. Then, about twenty minutes, later the rush of emotion left as quickly as it came. We left the church and went to the gravesite at Highland Cemetery, where her coffin was put onto the carriage pulled by the six white horses. It was the same cemetery where my grandparents, and most of my mother's family, rested.

Afterwards, we arrived at Mama's house to find the family members who had left the cemetery earlier, already filling their plates with the enormous amount of food that had been brought in to feed us. Someone turned on the television and to my amazement the movie "Imitation of Life" was being shown. I couldn't bring myself to watch it, but everyone else did, and when it got to the last scene, they understood why Mama wanted those white horses. It was eerie that her favorite movie was shown on the day of her funeral. It was almost as if she was there with us watching. In my spirit I could hear her saying to me, "It's okay now, Mike. I'm home. It's okay"

After the movie was over everyone started laughing and saying "Mama's still here. She's still in control."

I needed some space at that moment and went outside. I had walked only a short distance when my thoughts overtook me and I was once more reliving the final weeks that had brought me to this point in my life.

Suddenly I was back in North Carolina awaiting the beginning of the 2006 training camp. The Lord spoke to me and told me that I needed to take my boys, Michael and Isaiah, and visit my mama.

"Kim," I said. "I have to go. I don't know why I have such a strong feeling, but I need to go and take the boys with me."

"She's moving here in a month," Kim said. "Why is there such an urgency to travel all the way to Oklahoma?"

"I don't know, but we have to go," was the only explanation I could give her.

We flew out to Oklahoma and spent the whole time with Mama. It was the most peaceful visit I had ever had with her. I don't know if she knew what was about to happen, but I will never forget the visit. While the boys got a chance to be around their grandma and talk to her, I got an opportunity to enjoy her company once more, one-on-one. I had no idea it would be for the last time on earth.

As I reflect back, I believe that Mama's death was quite possibly the culmination of a series of events that took place over the last few years of her life. She had a brother and sister, with whom she was especially close. Her brother's name was Cleve Alexander and her sister's name was Loretta Stephenson. Uncle Cleve had been murdered a few years earlier when someone attempted to rob him at his house. By then, he had become very frail from years of alcohol abuse. Eventually, he had stopped drinking, but the toll on his body was too great. As a result, it's probable that he was unable to fight off his attacker who strangled him. His death was hard on Mama. Uncle Cleve had lived with us for much of my time at home and the relationship between he and my mama was extremely close.

Not long afterwards my Aunt Loretta was diagnosed with cancer. Both Mama and I had been very close to Aunt Loretta, because I had stayed with her a lot during my early years.

When Aunt Loretta passed away in 2004, my mom became very despondent. Soon afterwards, Mama went into the hospital suffering a light stroke. I suspect though, that her decline was brought on by the emotional effects of losing her brother and sister. She was there for an entire month.

That same year, Boo had a vision for a beauty salon in Charlotte. She was very excited and telephoned me to ask what I thought about it. The salon was to honor Mama by enabling other beauticians the opportunity to have their own business. I told her to e-mail me, but when she did, I did not respond right away.

One day, however, I was driving down the street and that's when it hit me that I needed to call Boo and get started on the salon. So I called her and said "Boo I'm ready to do the salon. God told me to fund your vision. Are you ready?"

Boo was still living in Lawton, Oklahoma at the time. She replied, "I've been ready."

Boo moved to Charlotte in 2005 and we began making plans for the salon. I remembered that when we were young, Chewy and I used to go to the salon where Mama worked and watch her. The whole idea came about from Boo's and my memories of Mama working to provide for her family, the best way she knew how.

Mama was very happy about the salon and wanted to move to Charlotte where she could be close to Boo and my family. So, before Boo moved to Charlotte in 2005, she promised Mama that once it was ready, she would bring her here to live.

After Boo left Lawton, Mama felt the loss of her family even more deeply. Out of her four children, only my brother Chewy remained in the area. I believe that despondency coupled with chronic diabetes, and the debilitating effects that her drinking had on her body over the years, was the cause of another hospital stay in 2005. During this time, she lapsed into a coma but revived.

In spite of my mama's precarious, health Boo and I both felt hopeful that once the salon was completed and we brought Mama here to live in the area, her health and spirit would be restored once again. We worked on the salon with that objective.

During a visit to Oklahoma in 2006, Mama asked Boo, "When are you going to come and get me?"

"It won't be until August," Boo replied. "I have a hair show I have to attend in Atlanta during the first weekend of August. Then I will come to Lawton and we'll drive back to Charlotte together. Mama was afraid to fly, so Boo had decided they would make the trip by car.

It was during that interim period in July that my boys and I were able to visit, which helped her pass the time while she was waiting for Boo to arrive.

Mama was scheduled to leave Oklahoma with Boo the weekend of August ninth and I was extremely happy that she would be living near us very soon. She would finally have the opportunity to be with her grandchildren as often as she wanted, and she would be able to see the salon that was built out of so much love, in her honor.

I was at training camp and Boo had just returned from Atlanta when the call from the hospital reached my sister. The doctor informed Boo that Mama had once again been admitted to the hospital but she was fine and he saw no reason that she would not be able to travel the following weekend. Although she was not able to speak with my mama at the time, Boo could hear her voice in the background speaking with a nurse. So, Boo saw no reason to be alarmed. She even asked the doctor if it would be better if she and my mama flew to Charlotte instead of making a tiring car trip.

"No, I don't think she will have a problem riding in the car," the doctor reassured Boo. "In fact, the trip and fresh air will probably be good for her," he continued.

Boo hung up the telephone and began to prepare for Mama's arrival. The next day Boo's daughter was moving her clothes to an upstairs bedroom so Mama could stay downstairs, when the telephone rang. It was the hospital calling to tell Boo that someone needed to come to Lawton immediately. Boo tried to explain that she had just talked with the doctor the day before and he had assured her that Mama was fine. Refusing to believe the situation had changed, Boo called the doctor.

"I don't know what happened," the doctor said. "She was fine. Then suddenly all her organs began to shut down. Someone needs to come immediately."

"What do you mean?" Boo asked.

"You need to come." the doctor repeated.

Boo hurriedly packed some clothes and headed for Charlotte's Douglas International Airport to catch any flight that would eventually get her to Oklahoma. It was already late at night and when she arrived she found that there was no flight available that left that late at night.

I was still at training camp when I got a phone call from my cousin who told me that I needed to come to Lawton. He repeated what he thought I already knew, that Mama was in the hospital and she was not doing well. I knew that Boo was on her way there and would call me with the details of what was happening. Then later that night, Boo called to tell me she could not get a flight out and asked for my help.

I went to the team chaplain Mike Bunkley and said, "I need to get to Oklahoma. Things are not looking good for my mama." Mike told me he would take care of it.

A short time later, the man who takes care of travel plans for the Panthers, called me with all the arrangements. The Panthers had arranged for me to fly out with Kim and Boo in a private plane. The next morning we left for Lawton.

When we arrived at the hospital, Mama was in a coma. Nevertheless, I reasoned that she had been like this the year before, but she had come out of it and was fine. I was hopeful this time it would be the same.

We arrived at the hospital at about 10 a.m. on Wednesday morning, and I spent the whole day with her praying and talking and reading scriptures to her. I talked to her saying, "Mama you have to come back." A little later that day, the doctor told me that her body was shutting down and she probably would not make it through the night. He needed to know if we wanted her to be put on life support. To have to make that decision about someone's life is extremely daunting, but I knew that Mama would not want that. When it was her time to pass, she wanted to go with dignity and with her family around her. So I told the doctor that we would not be putting her on life support.

Later that night, as I sat by her bedside, the Lord spoke to my heart and told me that she was not coming back this time. At that moment, I knew that Mama was gone. Lying in her bed was just her earthly body. It was really tough and I was so torn. I didn't want to believe it, but I know the Lord's voice when He talks to me and I knew what He had said would come to pass.

Around midnight we all left for the hotel, but almost as soon as we arrived, the hospital called to say we needed to come back if we wanted to see Mama before she passed away. Fortunately, we were only a short distance away and, as we walked back into her room and gathered around her bed, all the monitors went to 0. At 12:08 a.m. Thursday, August 10, 2006, Florida Maye Minter left us for a better place to live. She was gone and I was left alone once more to wonder about the true meaning of my life. I felt exactly like I did when I got hurt during my sophomore year at Nebraska. That night, the meaning of my life had flashed before me as I lay on that football field thinking that all my hopes and dreams had been destroyed in a single moment. I felt the same now, as I looked at my mama lying so still in that bed. I just couldn't believe it. Then all the emotion of what had just happened engulfed me, and I was hit with a multitude of feelings from crying to numbness.

After we said our goodbyes to Mama, I became focused on the funeral. I guess this was my way of dealing with the situation. I remembered that Mama had said she wanted the white horses to carry her coffin, just like in the movie "Imitation of Life," so I was determined to get those horses for her. I wanted my mama's funeral to be one that everyone in Lawton would never forget.

I explained the situation to a friend of mine and said, "We've got to find six white horses." We went all over Lawton and even to the military base at Fort Sill where we asked everyone that might know where we could find those horses. Finally we talked to someone at the rodeo in Lawton and they made the contacts. Then someone called and said we can get those horses for you but they have to come from California. They're going to be expensive. I said "I don't care. Just get those horses."

So the horses arrived a day or two later along with the carriage where the coffin would rest. Then a cousin of mine said, "Mike, we need to take her through the center of Lawton and down the streets where we grew up."

I wondered how we were going to get permission to take a casket through the city. So I called the police station to find out where I could get permission. Finally we received approval and in the same manner that any distinguished person might have been transported through the town, Mama rode in her carriage. The onlookers stood in silence or waved, as the passing hearse evoked all sorts of memories for loved ones now departed.

At last, it was finally over. All of the hurrying and arranging of the past few days was finished. Soon everyone would return to their normal lives, but mine would never be the same. I had crossed into uncharted territory and I felt as if I was a ship, trying desperately to maneuver in rough waters without a sextant or compass.

I suppose I should have known that I would probably outlive Mama. That's usually they way it works out, but I had never really given it that much thought. She was always there for me, and I guess in the back of my mind, I thought that it would always be like that. Yet, here I was, for the first time in my life, without her, and I just couldn't seem to come to grips with how I would handle this change in my life.

I reflected again on Mama's life and realized that the majority of it was spent trying to make the best existence possible for her four children. She had worked hard and had made a home for us. Yes, we were poor and did without a lot of material things that other children had, but we never felt unwanted or uncared for, and we always had a place we could call our home. Her choices were clear to me. She preferred her family over her own dreams and ambitions. That realization suddenly became a beacon for me about my own attitudes towards my wife and my children.

Then, just as God had done so many times in my life, He gently reminded me that He is the source of the strength in my life, not Mama. Although my love for her will never diminish, it is God who sustains me through the anguish of losing her. There is no person or power on earth that can substitute for the love that God wants to shower on His people. With Him, through His Son, Jesus, all things are possible. All hurt can be healed, and dreams that one might never believe possible, can be fulfilled. I felt relieved, and I understood that I had not been set adrift with no direction. I was firmly anchored to a God who would always be there to comfort and guide me through the most challenging moments of my life.

That day, I walked back to Mama's house for the last time. I had passed a milestone in my life. I would never be the same again.

I do not know how I could have faced the following year without my faith in a God that is greater then any circumstance I would encounter. His constant comfort and influence has been the most deciding factor in my ability to overcome the most discouraging times in my life. Jesus Christ carried every fear and hurt in my life and replaced them with peace and joy that is beyond expression. I could have never achieved any of my goals without my faith in His ability to lead wherever His plan for my life took me.

This is a story about living a dream, but that dream can be different for each individual person. It's not about football, or making a lot of money. A lot of money can't make you happy. Money only brings different circumstances and responsibilities that can be just as hard as not having enough money. Perhaps that is the reason why so many people, who win the lottery, are broke just a few years later. True happiness only comes from knowing who you really are, and where you are going when you leave this earthly body. It can't be purchased or earned. It's a gift.

That's why there is also no better place in this book to tell others about my wife, Kim, and how much she has been a help and support to me. Her dedication to me and our family is an inspiration and a role model for how I want our children to remember their mother.

When I met Kim we were both teenagers ourselves, each of us having our own dreams for the future. Yet, once Kim and I fell in love and were married, she began to understand what being an NFL wife was all about. For ten years she has waited patiently at home with our children while I was away almost every weekend part of the year. Her greatest desire was to keep our family nucleus solid and secure. To accomplish that very important task, she stayed away from the spotlight and put her own dreams on hold. It was a sacrifice that many NFL wives are unwilling to make. She has truly played a very active part of making my dream come true. For giving me that gift, I will be forever grateful to her.

My children complete my life and I love family time. When Kim sees me playing with our children, she's happy. We call Michael our bionic son because he is always on the move and clowning around. He is the one that tests our patience more than all of the other children. Yet, he excels in his athletic skills. Isaiah is more like I was as a child. He's serious when he needs to be but he knows how to have fun, too. Brianna is the child that is solidly rooted to the ground and weighs circumstances as if her life depended on each decision she makes. Brianna is the caretaker, in the family, like her mother. McKenna looks at life like she doesn't have a care in the world. She would probably jump off a house before she even thought twice about it. How can four children, raised in one family have such different personalities? My family is another blessing that God has given to me.

My career in professional football finally ended before the 2007 season began, and at 33-years-old, it appeared that I would need to begin reinventing myself. I thought about this fact one day as I sat in my office. It wasn't as though I hadn't made any plans for the future. I had set up some after football business interests. But still, I had to wonder how a relatively young, professional athlete could reposition himself to fit into a modern day world. I had so much more to give of myself, but to whom, and how?

GOD ISN'T FINISHED WITH ME YET!

"An individual has not started living until he can rise above the narrow confines of his individualistic concerns to the broader concerns of all humanity." Martin Luther King, Jr.

I grew up in an area of Lawton where there was a church practically on every corner, yet the crime and use of drugs and alcohol was rampant. Even though segregation in schools was suspended long before I was born, it hadn't changed the mindset of the people of Lawton, both blacks and whites. The blacks stayed in their areas of the town and the white people had their particular streets. Neither group preferred to cross that invisible barrier, unless there was a necessity to do so. I suppose it's true that you can change the law with the stroke of a pen, but you can't change people's hearts quite so easily.

When people segregate themselves from each other, it creates an environment in which fear and animosity develop. That leads to anger and the anger usually leads to violence. I remember when I was growing up how fear of the police among the black people was prevalent. Even as a young child, I felt that the police were always following me and out to get me. As a boy whenever I walked in a store, I sensed that I was being watched or followed.

When I was older, the use of crack cocaine was added to the culture, and gangs began to develop. I started to notice that people I had looked up to had become addicted. Beautiful girls that I went to school with and even dated had become old, far beyond their years, as the need for drugs and sex became the driving force in their lives. I saw so many great athletes with sharp minds whose lives were destroyed due to alcohol and drugs, before they were even given a chance to shine. The wisdom of old men was disregarded because their affinity for the bottle gave people the perspective that they had nothing valuable to say.

I am sad to admit that many of my own family went to prison for a variety of crimes. Yet I am here today as an example of a person that grew up in that same environment, struggling to obtain every conceivable benefit that life could offer a poor child from the black community.

This is one reason why back in the 1960's that Malcolm X and the Black Muslims and the other so-called "power groups" were able to get the attention of black people. The people identified with those groups because they were really hurting and in pain. These power groups spoke to the black people and changed their minds about education. In theory, they were giving people something that was good. These groups related to their pain and gave the people something good that would help them get from where they were at, to where they were going. That's why the people wanted to believe in them. That's why the movements that occurred during the 1960's and 1970's became so well established and accepted among the black community.

But where did it all begin? How did we get through 200 years of history in this country with so little progress? Even today, with all the emphasis there is on helping minority groups, we are still looking at an astronomical rate of black on black murders, gang involvement with our young people and a socio-economic level that continues to be substandard to the majority of the white community.

To understand this a little more I believe you have to look back at the history of the black people in the United States. Africans were kidnapped and enslaved and then brought to this country over 200 years ago. At that time families were torn apart and family units were broken up. The whole purpose of these white slavers was to multiply the blacks by breeding them. At this time, a black man was supposed to go into every hut and make babies. They were not encouraged to have any ties or relationships. The man's job was simply to work and create more labor force for the white landowners. The mother's job was to take care of those babies. Today, that same mindset is prevalent in black culture. The man in the family is still missing.

The continuing impact of this goes on from generation to generation. Black kids didn't go to white neighborhoods and visa versa. In white neighborhoods, kids grew up in a family environment. Television only epitomized what white families believed. They were engulfed in a world of "Father Knows Best" and "Leave it to Beaver," because there was stability to it all. On the other hand, in black neighborhoods, we were learning that what you were supposed to do is have sex with as many girls as you can. That's why it's so easy for white kids to grow up believing in being married to one person. This environment even reinforces the fact that you should stay in a marriage where you aren't happy. The traditional white culture promotes the ideal family as a marriage to one spouse for life. Even though that seems to be less the case presently, isn't that really a step backwards?

In my own life, I can look back and see that same mindset and influence during my formative years. Now that I have children of my own I see many things differently. But, when I was 15, the things I did were influenced by my culture. Consequently, there was a girl that I was involved with when I was 15 and in the 10th grade. She got pregnant with my baby. I remember her parents sitting down and talking to us about what had happened. Even then I realized that her pregnancy was a consequence of a decision I had made and I was ready to deal with it. They made her have an abortion. But I still remember sitting there and saying that I didn't agree with it. But that's what you did in my neighborhood. You were supposed to have girls and sex early. It's what made you tough and a man in the neighborhood. The goal was to see how many girls you could find to have sex with. That's how we grew up.

That decision could have affected my whole life. Later, I had people who claimed they had my baby. However, when they were tested, we found out that the claim wasn't valid. But it could have affected my whole life. I believe God protected me from a lot of things that could have happened. I could easily have had five or six kids. We didn't have a dad sitting down with us, telling us how to treat a woman. What we learned was how you become a player, how to be a pimp.

That's what happened to my sister Lynn, and as a result, she got caught up in prostitution. Initially, pimping was big in the 1970's and 1980's in Lawton. Those were the guys that had the Cadillacs. Then, the prostitution ring was moved to Texas in the late 1980's and that's why Lynn ended up there. Later, the best way to make a fast buck became drugs, and now it's almost all drugs. That was so-called progress-pimping to drugs, and all for fast money.

Now I'm not saying that the cycle can't be broken. What I'm saying is that for over 200 years, a majority of black people were slaves and conditioned to act in a particular way. Then we were freed. Yet, even when the black people were freed they really weren't free. What happened was that the black man was no longer a slave to another man, but he wasn't educated about the responsibility that freedom brings. Abraham Lincoln just said "You're free." He didn't say let me educate you on what freedom or family means, because for 200 years you've been taught one way and now we expect you to get into society and understand how to live a different lifestyle.

It didn't really begin to happen until the 1960's, so we're only talking about forty or fifty years of change. I believe there is a correlation here and until we get to the root of the problem, you can never solve it. It isn't enough to simply say "you should know better by now."

I believe looking at the neighborhoods today there is still a vast difference between the way the whites and blacks are taught and how kids grow up. No one ever sat down with me and said "Mike, you're supposed to get married and have a wife, take care of your family and that's what you're supposed to do. No one ever told me that and I didn't see it. It isn't obvious to people in a black community like it is in a white one.

Generally speaking, in a white community you see parents living together, working together and building a family. White kids see that as an example. You turn on the television and what do you see? You see two white parents together raising a family. Until the "The Jeffersons" and the "Bill Cosby Show" you never saw a black, educated family on television. That's what Bill Cosby was attacking. He was trying to provide positive images to our kids, because what black kids still see in most black families is a mom and kids with dad gone.

How do we overcome that? I only overcame it through Jesus Christ and His grace. He taught me that. The Bible taught me that. That's why I know the Holy Spirit is real, because He became my dad and He told me what to do. Did I make mistakes along the way? Absolutely, I did. But He was there to teach me how to become a father. In fact that was my first question to Him when my son, Michael, was born. "How do I become a father to him?"

This is so ironic, because I almost became a Black Muslim, and now I understand how black people can become converted so easily to that faith. It's because of the pain and the hurt that they have gone through. It because the Muslim religion adapts itself better to the culture of the black people, then the white Christian religion does.

I went to Africa several years ago and while I was there, I could feel the spirits of black people through the centuries. I saw, in my own spirit, the families that were brought into the courtyard. They were chained up to each other and the slave buyers were saying "I like that one and let me take that one." I thought at the time, this is crazy. I saw their spirits crying out saying, "No, don't take me! Don't do me like this."

I have to admit that, until I was able to turn my feelings over to God, I did not like white people. I believed strongly that white people just didn't get it. They didn't take seriously the pain that the black people had been through and they didn't really want to understand it. The funny thing about all this is that I married a white woman. But I didn't begin to like white people in general, until I met her family. This is the way I was, until I met Kim's family and got an opportunity to sit down and talk with them and be around them.

Until then, the only white people I liked were the ones that played on my team because the team kind of took away the cultural divisiveness of peoples' lives. Today, I tell people that, on a team when people come in with one common goal, it doesn't matter what you look like or believe. If they are all focused on one goal, they can accomplish anything they desire to do. I know that for a fact, because when I was growing up, we had some kids on my teams who were absolute racists, and I was one of them. Some kids were poor and some rich, and some had two parents and some were with foster parents. Some kids were smart and others not so intelligent, but when we all came together we were one.

Then, I got saved through Jesus Christ, and God began to show me that it isn't about white or black. It's about sin and ignorance. It's about blindness.

God showed me that when they hanged His Son on a cross, it wasn't about hatred, it was about blindness. They just didn't see. Now when I am with someone who is outwardly prejudiced, I never look at that person as having hatred. I look at them as being blinded. When I see a person like that I think, you need to see the light, because when you do, you will understand that it isn't about hate, it's about God's people. When I look at people now, I'd like to think that I see what God sees. I see their spirits and the greatness in them. This is why I believe that I can relate to people when others can't. If you can nourish that greatness in people, it's impossible to stop it. This is why I'm a firm believer that God is sending me places that I never thought I would be going. I know that God is going to use me to do something beyond what I have already accomplished.

He first showed me in college, but I got scared. I thought at the time, I want to play football. That's what I really want to do. I prayed God please don't take me on this mission that I believe you want me to go on because I just want to play football. So I backed away for a while. I backed away from the Word, and I backed away from everything He wanted for me to do.

My senior year, we were playing Michigan and I was having a great game. I had just stopped an interception and suddenly I was aware of God's greatness...right there on the field. It so overwhelmed to me that I was lying on the field and put my face to the ground and said to Him, "God I can't take it. Please don't show me anymore. I just can't do it." I understand why in the Bible someone would fall face down when they were in God's presence, because I know what being in His presence and what His greatness is like.

Athletics proved to be my way of maintaining a focus on my life and it led me to the successes that I have achieved so far. However, while my abilities allowed me the opportunity play football at the highest level, it was not the path through which satisfaction and happiness in my life was reached.

I think back to my days at the University of Nebraska and my mindset before I met Joshua Molachek. Through him, I was touched by the courage of a young boy who knew Jesus. Until that time I really thought that football was the beginning and end, the Alpha and Omega of my life. I truly believed that without the opportunity to play the game, I could never be happy. Yet, it wasn't until that opportunity was almost taken away from me that I learned that the only true happiness I have ever known was when I came to know Jesus Christ and the power that He has to transform each of our lives.

However, I am also aware of the basic needs and desires of individuals to work and support their families. Nevertheless, because of a variety of circumstances, many low income families need help to reach that level.

There is an old adage, "Give a man a fish and you feed him for one day. Teach a man to fish and you feed him for a lifetime." Unfortunately, many of the support systems instituted by the government today have created a dependence on government subsistence. Those who are forced to use that venue to survive, become so established in it that they never leave. That heritage is passed to their children and grandchildren producing a culture of people who are never ever able to break that vicious self-fulfilling cycle. I am happy to say that Mama never chose that route in order to support her family.

God has placed in me a determination to erase that dangerous trend in the United States. I believe that awareness of the problem is only part of the solution. The other part lays in manner in which we solve it.

I am reminded of a story I once heard about the manner in which the communist government was able to bring the people of Lithuania under its control. When the soldiers first marched into the country to subdue it, it was not with tanks and guns. Their first act of conquest was to prevent the churches from offering help to the poor. Instead they required that any person, who needed assistance, received it from government sources. Once the poor were under the government's control, then the next stage was to replace priests and ministers in the churches with those who were sympathetic to the government position. The True Church was forced underground. Those courageous people knew full well that the threat of death hung over the heads of any individuals who dared to disobey the government's directive, which stated that it was illegal to congregate together. As a result, the needs of the people grew and the ability to provide for that need diminished until the day Lithuania was again out from under communist domination.

My point in relating this story is not to suggest that the United States is in any way subversive with its methods of subsidizing the poor. It is simply to say that without God, the help given will never be enough to sustain the growing need.

I believe that God has called me to be a bridge by helping the white culture to better understand other cultures, so they can work together to achieve a greatness that the United States of America can represent proudly to the world.

I also believe that God is directing me to help other people, no matter what their race, creed or color, to rise above even their most challenging circumstances, in order to achieve the dream that each individual has in his or her life. How I will be involved is in God's hands, but I know that in order for it to be truly successful, God must be involved in the process.

I never knew my grandfather, since he passed away five years before I was born. So it's amazing to me that I would be so much like him. My grandfather was a preacher and the same fire that was inside of him is in me. I don't know whether or not DNA and genetics influenced certain aspects of our natures. I do know that I possess the same zeal and ability that my grandfather had to speak to people, and tell them about my experience with Jesus.

It is my hope that people reading about my life, will begin to understand that it is only through knowing Jesus Christ and the power of His love that a person can ever be completely fulfilled. This happiness and enjoyment of life is available to everyone. It isn't distributed by income, race or knowledge. It is given freely and in abundance as a gift to anyone to who asks for it.

My challenge to everyone who reads this book is simply to ask for Jesus to be a part of your life and to believe that He is real. Life may fail you and you may believe you are at the end of your rope, but no matter how far you have fallen, you can never fall out of the reach of God's hand.

Printed in the United States
127448LV00003B/154-999/P